MARCEL PROUST

In the same series:

Leonid Andreyev *Josephine M. Newcombe*

Isaac Babel *R. W. Hallett*

Saul Bellow *Brigitte Scheer-Schäzler*

Bertolt Brecht *Willy Haas*

Albert Camus *Carol Petersen*

Willa Cather *Dorothy Tuck McFarland*

Colette *Robert Cottrell*

John Dos Passos *George J. Becker*

Theodore Dreiser *James Lundquist*

Friedrich Dürrenmatt *Armin Arnold*

T. S. Eliot *Joachim Seyppel*

William Faulkner *Joachim Seyppel*

Max Frisch *Carol Petersen*

Robert Frost *Elaine Barry*

Maksim Gorki *Gerhard Habermann*

Gunter Grass *Kurt Lothar Tank*

Peter Handke *Nicholas Hern*

Ernest Hemingway *Samuel Shaw*

Hermann Hesse *Franz Baumer*

Uwe Johnson *Mark Boulby*

James Joyce *Armin Arnold*

Franz Kafka *Franz Baumer*

Sinclair Lewis *James Lundquist*

Georg Lukács *Ehrhard Bahr and Ruth Goldschmidt Kunzer*

Thomas Mann *Arnold Bauer*

Alberto Moravia *Jane E. Cottrell*

Vladimir Nabokov *Donald E. Morton*

Eugene O'Neill *Horst Frenz*

José Ortega y Gasset *Franz Niedermayer*

George Orwell *Roberta Kalechofsky*

Katherine Anne Porter *John Edward Hardy*

Ezra Pound *Jeannette Lander*

Rainer Maria Rilke *Arnold Bauer*

Jean-Paul Sartre *Liselotte Richter*

Isaac Bashevis Singer *Irving Malin*

Thornton Wilder *Hermann Stresau*

Thomas Wolfe *Fritz Heinrich Ryssel*

Virginia Woolf *Manly Johnson*

Richard Wright *David Bakish*

Modern Literature Monographs

MARCEL PROUST

James Robert Hewitt

Frederick Ungar Publishing Co.
New York

Copyright © 1975 by Frederick Ungar Publishing Co., Inc.
Printed in the United States of America
Library of Congress Catalog Card Number: 74-76127
Designed by Anita Duncan
ISBN: 0-8044-2382-2

For Robert K. Bishop
my first teacher

Contents

Chronology ix

1 The Magic-Lantern World 1

2 Prisoners of Illusion 27

3 A Masked Ball 55

4 The Light in the Window 73

5 The Dandy and the Monk 89

Bibliography 113

Index 117

Chronology

1871:   10 July: Marcel Proust is born in the Auteuil section of Paris

1880:   Suffers his first asthma attack

1882-89:   Studies at the Lycée Condorcet; spends vacations at Illiers

1889-90:   Does military service at Orléans

1892-93:   Becomes a frequent figure in Parisian society. Publishes stories and articles in periodicals

1894:   Visits Norman coast for summer vacation

Begins an attachment with composer Reynaldo Hahn

1896:   *Pleasures and Regrets* is published, with an introduction by Anatole France

1896-99:   Devotes himself to writing a novel, *Jean Santeuil*

1900:   Visits Venice

1900-03:   Studies and translates art critic John Ruskin

1903:   Proust's father dies

1904:   Publishes his translation of Ruskin's *The Bible at Amiens*. Contributes articles on Paris society to the newspaper *Le Figaro*

1905:   Proust's mother dies; he enters a health sanitarium

1907:   Contributes to *Le Figaro*. Engages Alfred Agostinelli as his chauffeur

1908:   Starts work on a book of literary criticism, attacking the critical methods of Sainte-Beuve

1909:   Retreats from the social world to write *Swann's Way*

1912:   Re-engages Agostinelli as his secretary. Seeks a publisher for his novel

1913:   *Swann's Way*, volume one of *Remembrance of Things Past*, is published at Proust's own expense

1914:   Agostinelli dies in an airplane crash; Proust is grief-stricken

1914-18: Continues to work on his novel intensely, correcting and greatly augmenting the text

1918:   *Within a Budding Grove* is published

1919:   Proust is awarded the coveted Goncourt Prize for fiction

1920:   First part of *The Guermantes Way* is published

1921:   Second part of *The Guermantes Way* and first part of *Cities of the Plain* are published

1922:   Second part of *Cities of the Plain* is published. 18 November: Marcel Proust dies in Paris

1923:   *The Captive* is published

1925:   *The Sweet Cheat Gone* is published

1927:   *The Past Recaptured*, seventh and last volume of *Remembrance of Things Past*, is published

1952:   Manuscript pages of Proust's first novel, *Jean Santeuil*, are edited and published

1954:   Manuscript pages of Proust's Sainte-Beuve essay (*On Art and Literature*) are edited and published

1971:   Centennial of Proust's birth is marked internationally

----

The English titles of Proust's seven-volume novel, *A la recherche du temps perdu*, are those of the standard translation by C. K. Scott Moncrief and Frederick Blossom, published as *Remembrance of Things Past* (in two volumes) by Random House. Translations within the text of this study are those of the author.

The Magic-Lantern World

The writer's work is but an optical instrument
through which the reader may see within himself.
—M.P.

For centuries, the devout and the sightseer have been making the pilgrimage to Chartres, fifty miles or so southwest of Paris, to visit its splendid medieval cathedral. In recent decades, a new breed of pilgrim has discovered and sanctified a shrine in the nearby village of Illiers: the former vacation home of Marcel Proust's family, a site that he lovingly and meticulously detailed in *Remembrance of Things Past*. The town of Illiers, rechristened Combray by the novelist, is undistinguished in itself, indistinguishable from countless similar hamlets of the French countryside, and is easy to bypass. It has become, however, one of the most imposing geographical creations in the world of fiction.

Marcel Proust, who believed in the reality of art—and quite literally gave his life to art—would probably not have been surprised at the great numbers of "Proustians" who have made this pilgrimage (particularly during 1971, the centenary of his birth). Nor by the still vaster number of readers who have never heard of Illiers and firmly accept the reality of the fictional Combray. For Combray is far more than the prototype of a nineteenth-century country town; it is the universe of the imagination that each of us frequents as a child.

Reduced to its simplest outline, *Remembrance of Things Past* is the story of a boy growing up in the last quarter of that century. As he reaches maturity, he finds his dreams to be illusions and his life a handful of dust. How he regains "time lost," recaptures the past and discovers the meaning and value of his life, provides Proust's novel with one of the most dramatically original climaxes in fiction.

Aside from the scenes of early childhood at Combray, some of the most striking episodes in the novel deal with a stratum of society quite alien to us today. The Parisian *gratin*, literally meaning "upper crust," consisted of a number of authentically old aristocratic families that had doggedly survived revolution and change, gloriously persisting into the Third Republic, rooted in that section of Paris called the Faubourg St. Germain.

A veritable caste system prevailed, following an intricate pattern of title, prestige and protocol. Family ties were strong, but pride and social ambition often stronger. It was a world where cousin cut cousin. Virtually every noblewoman maintained a salon—literary, artistic or purely social—and the exclusivity of her salon bore witness to her rank and power. Within that rigid system lay the visible strength of the aristocracy, but also its vulnerability. For they were increasingly imitated by the untitled, ambitious nouveau riche. Through a display of grandeur and by courting "names," a wealthy bourgeoise could create the illusion of prestige. The caste-conscious Parisian public soon lost the distinction between parvenus and established nobility.

This was a world Proust knew well. Son of a prosperous bourgeois family, he was not born to the Faubourg but, gifted with native charm and adept in the social graces, he was one of countless dandyish young men of the period who inevitably maneuvered the "right" invitations. As a very young man, the colorful plumage of the Faubourg exercised its spell on him. But he was more particularly fascinated by its studied manners and inherent *snobisme*. With maturity, he achieved the detachment to chronicle that brief gaudy moment of social history with exceptional insight. It is inadequate, however, to see Proust's novel solely in terms of its social panorama. Though the book can be read, and should be read, in terms of history, sociology, psychology, philosophy, it is primarily a personal and spiritual quest.

The design of *Remembrance of Things Past* is monumental. While the essence of a life may sometimes be richly recaptured with brevity (as in Flaubert's short story, *A Simple Heart*), Proust chose the luxury of length. His novel, one of the longest ever written, is sustained through the simple but ever-compelling narrative device of the first person "I."

We are not, however, projected totally into the past as we usually are in first-person novels; rather, the past is brought forward and re-experienced. Proust succeeded in maintaining a subtle equilibrium wherein the reader alternately, or sometimes even simultaneously, perceives past events as they seemed then and as they seem now. Never actually leaving the present confines of the narrator's mind, we move freely, imperceptibly, backward and forward in time, trespassing on a varied geography where a myriad of characters live, love, die, and make fools of themselves.

The work is divided into seven volumes, each having the length and substance of a novel in itself. It is essential, however, for a clear understanding of Proust's intention, to recognize that this is a single, prolonged excursion of the mind, not a series of separate, interconnected entities that the French call a *roman fleuve* (such as Jules Romains's *Men of Good Will* or Galsworthy's *Forsythe Saga*). Nor is it, as people erroneously continue to believe, a *roman à clef*, that bastard genre in which characters under fictitious names are readily recognizable to those holding the "key." While a number of the principals in Proust's novel may be traced to Proust's circle of notable acquaintances, each character is essentially, as in any significant work of art, a composite. Proust's biographer, George Painter, has performed ambitious detective work in tracking the originals of certain characters, and while his discoveries sometimes make for racy reading, we are, in the long run, no better equipped to appreciate the richness and depth of ideas that form the true matter of the novel. Proust wanted us to recognize in his characters people whom *we* know, not merely those he had known. Even the first-person narrator does not correspond to Proust himself. While drawing heavily from his own experiences, and more heavily still from his store of philosophical observations, he has nonetheless contrived a fictional self to represent him on the stage of his novel, which is not, in the literal sense, autobiographical. I have reserved a discussion of the resemblances between Marcel Proust and the Narrator Marcel (as critics have traditionally come to call him) for the end of this study when the reader is more familiar with the character of the protagonist.

Although "remembrance of things past" is perhaps best known today as the title of this epic French novel, its source is profoundly English, Proust's translator having borrowed the phrase from one of Shakespeare's more tender sonnets: "When from the sessions of sweet silent thought/ I summon up remembrance of things past. . . ." While the translation of such a vast work represents a stupendous achievement, one to which C. K. Scott Moncrief consecrated his life, *Remembrance of Things Past* fails to capture the connotations of the original *A la recherche du temps perdu,* literally "in search of time lost."*

The novel is indeed a vast reminiscence, the record and reconstruction of a single life, encompassing at the same time the history of an era and its society. Yet the underlying theme of Proust's novel, which is a desperate and haunting search, the pursuit of a pattern of meaning, is unfortunately not suggested by such a delicate, rose-tinted word as our English "remembrance."

Proust's work is far more than mere *mémoires,* far more than the decline and fall of a social hierarchy; it represents one man's struggle to understand himself and those whose lives had touched his, an attempt to give meaning to that complex mystery which is his own life. At the heart of the complexity and mystery, Proust sensed the problem of time, time that brings changes with each hour, each day, and constantly alters our relationships with others. He was inter-

---

* Proust knew just enough English to protest, unsuccessfully. He also preferred *Le temps perdu* (time lost) to the more elaborate title insisted on by his French editors. In this instance, one may judge him wrong.

ested in the processes of human memory, their function both
in and apart from the realm of chronological time. Above
all, he was concerned with the possibility of a reality outside
time, the possibility of man's release from the bondage of
time's erosion which ends in death. But the extra-temporal
reality he sought lay within a human framework, devoid of
the crutch of theology or mysticism.

When the first volume appeared in 1913, many readers
were baffled and rebuffed. The French spirit is intolerant of
apparent chaos. Yet readers and critics with insight not only
found majesty in the style but intuitively detected the blue-
print of a massive architectural design, although few could
perceive the total shape the completed structure would assume. One problem, other than the book's leisurely length,
still sometimes troubles today's reader. Proust rejects conventional chronology. To acknowledge time as such would
have been antithetical to his purpose. We must refrain from
wondering whether the Narrator is ten or twelve, fifteen or
sixteen years old in particular episodes, and accept them as
symbolic of childhood or of adolescence. Also, Proust consciously had his Narrator's mind leap backward and forward, reconstructing his life in what deceptively seems random fashion. This is not the interior monologue developed
in later fiction, but a controlled network of analogies and
superimposed tableaux, devoid of stylistic distortions. While
Proust's work achieves effects comparable to those of James
Joyce or Gertrude Stein, his style, though adventurous and
innovative, is nonetheless grounded in the syntactical strength
of centuries of French prose.

If the Narrator, late in the novel and presumably an
adult, seems unduly preoccupied with memories of his
mother's goodnight kiss, this is more than a Freudian obsession, it is a conscious artistic effort to reproduce, in time
present, events remembered with all the vivid actuality of
their original impression. It is this *simultaneity* of past-in-

present, a bold departure from traditional metaphysics and aesthetics, that is distinctively Proustian.

The literary climate in which Marcel Proust grew up was intensely active, varied, and contradictory in its tendencies. Proponents of the symbolist movement sought to create "music" in both poetry and prose, believed it the writer's task to discover the rare and miraculous that lay beyond reality. This was a strongly subjective literature. Meanwhile, Zola and the naturalist writers were proposing an objective, scientific detachment in recording "reality as is." They favored a brutally frank, photographic approach to the squalid lives of the masses or the raw existence of whores, alcoholics, and the like. This was a world, and an aesthetic point of view, that had no appeal to Proust the writer. And while symbolism was destined to leave its mark on his work, he turned elsewhere, to the past, for his eclectic choice of models.

Throughout Proust's novel there are recurring references to three particular works; he is clearly calling our attention to them in terms of his own design. The first is Balzac's *Comédie Humaine,* an aggregate of over seventy novels collectively embracing all segments of Parisian and provincial life during the early nineteenth century. Balzac's most genial inspiration was carrying key characters from book to book, thereby reinforcing the unity and panoramic sweep of his vast *Comédie.* Marcel Proust, though writing a single novel with a more modest social focus, sought to capture a Balzacian vision of mankind. In the manner of Balzac, his characters disappear and reappear until such time as their lives, with the Narrator's, are recaptured on one great canvas, disparate pieces of a puzzle seen as a uniform structural whole.

While seeking breadth and scope, Proust also exercised his memorialist's genius for minutiae. In this, he emulated the Duc de Saint-Simon, whose massive *Mémoires* record in vivid detail the court life under Louis XIV, with penetrating portraits of its scheming courtiers. Thus, Proust often narrows his lens to seize, beyond overt action and reaction, each telling gesture, the glance and tone of voice that reveal the inner psychology of his characters.

Scattered, indeed sowed, throughout his novel are also allusions to a very different work, that wondrous fantasy, the *Arabian Nights*. At Combray, the Narrator recalls a set of family dishes, each of which depicts a scene from the *Thousand and One Nights*. Throughout his life, when people or places suddenly emerge in an unexpected metamorphosis, he speaks of them as though touched by a "magician's wand." In the final volume, *The Past Recaptured,* he describes a strange new Paris mysteriously transformed into a scene from an oriental tale. He begins to see his own life as a fantastic saga of "a thousand and one nights." It is Proust's way of alerting us that within the richly detailed patterns of a great thick tapestry, hidden truths lie subtly woven, that a book may be a magic carpet taking us outside human space and time.

The most celebrated episode of Proust's novel, the scene that serves as its "prime mover," has something of the enchanted aura of the *Arabian Nights*. By way of introduction to his reminiscences, the Narrator tells how difficult it is for one's *intellect* to recapture with fidelity our impressions of places and people or the immediate intensity of emotions. He undergoes an experience of memory that acts as a kind of magic carpet. While dipping a *madeleine* cake into a cup of tea, he is suddenly catapulted back into the world of his childhood where he first experienced that same sensation: the smell and the steam of the tea, the shape and the texture of the pastry, the crumbs floating on the surface of the liquid, opening out like Japanese flower petals, their taste against his palate. Miraculously outside time, a world lost is resurrected: "so that in that very moment, all the flowers in our garden, all the flowers in M. Swann's park and the water lilies of the Vivonne River, the good people of the village, their little homes and the church, the whole of Combray and its surroundings, all this came forth with shape and solidity, town, gardens and everything, from my cup of tea."

The World of Combray. Although the Narrator does paint a verbal picture of this town in which he spent his Easter holidays as a boy, he is more particularly interested in something very different from picturesque physical description; he is concerned with the portrayal of human behavior and the reconstruction of childhood dreams. The household at Combray consists of Marcel's maternal grandparents and a covey of dotty aunts, one of whom is conspicuously eccentric. Aunt Léonie, to whom this house belongs, is the classic imaginary invalid who has retreated to her room, jealously demanding attentions, chattering softly to herself (in order to keep her blood circulating), looking out the window to keep contact with the world, and entertaining two regular visitors who keep her further apprised of that world.

Nor is Aunt Léonie the only one who observes a mechanically rigid routine of existence; she is symbolic of life at Combray, which, while agreeable enough for a vacationing youngster, is utterly devoid of variety or adventure, stifled by what Proust calls the "anesthesia of habit." Although the meals are imaginatively, even artistically prepared by his aunt's chief servant, Françoise, they follow a strict pattern. The assembled family repeats the same cliché compliments, the same speculations on the weather, conforms in today's behavior to yesterday's and tomorrow's. One exception to this rigorous household timetable is that the Saturday lunch is scheduled an hour earlier than it is on other days. Yet even this deviation from the norm, this "assymetrical

Saturday," is assimilated as the variation that completes the pattern.

One "escape" from household routine is provided by walks in the rural environs of Combray, yet this, too, comes to follow a prescribed code. The family's decision as to which path to take on a particular day (and hence by which door of the house to leave) is dependent on the weather. For one walk is longer than the other, and threatening skies dictate the shorter of the two. To the child Marcel, both paths tentatively hold mystery and adventure of a kind, because they embody the inaccessible. "Swann's Way" refers to the road leading to the neighboring village of Méséglise. It is called this because one passes, en route, the home of M. Swann, an old family friend. One does not visit there, however, for Swann has married beneath him, and unspoken protocol forbids social contact with the "notorious" Odette Swann. "The Guermantes Way" is equally forbidding, for there one nears the unapproachable estate of one of the oldest and noblest of French titled families.

In moral terms, of which the boy is but fuzzily aware, these paths respectively represent a "low" road and a "high" road out from the confines of Combray—worlds which excite his childish imagination but with which he sees no possibility of direct communion. He senses a still more distinct dichotomy between the two since the family walks never take a circular sweep. Instead they follow the direct line from home to a particular point, then back via the same "way." Both, then, are essentially promenades without destination. In the Narrator's juvenile geography, it is inconceivable that the two paths might somewhere, somehow meet.

If his Aunt Léonie has made of herself a voluntary prisoner in her room, we may consider the boy Marcel as a sometime prisoner in his own room. After dinner, he would go to bed, and the sense of isolation he felt there would be redeemed only by his mother's good-night kiss. But often this embrace was denied him if company arrived. "Company" at Combray was invariably M. Swann, whose elegance, culture, and breeding make it hard to believe that he could have married a former *cocotte*. (She does not, of course, accompany her husband on these calls.) Swann is what we commonly call a "man of the world," widely traveled, frequenting the best society, and a connoisseur of the arts. His arrival, announced by a little bell at the garden gate, is, for Marcel, ambivalent. It is Swann who brings the magic and mystery of unknown worlds into the boy's humdrum existence, yet it is also Swann's visit that often deprives him of the good-night kiss, that symbol of maternal affection on which he is dependent.

Swann's presence thus embraces the themes of love and art: like a messenger from the outside world, he disrupts the comfortable routine of daily life with the prospect of distant enchantment. He tells the boy about museums and cathedrals, shows him pictures of Venice and Florence; so steeped in artistic lore is Swann that he sees ordinary life about him in terms of paintings. When he refers to the pregnant kitchen maid as "Giotto's Charity," Marcel is enraptured and mystified.

As the boy grows up, Swann becomes a kind of mentor, providing access to many of the worlds of his childhood dreams. The very name Swann suggests a miraculous fairy-tale bird that might carry a youngster over calm limpid waters from port to enchanted port. It is Swann's daughter Gilberte with whom Marcel later becomes infatuated. More than just a pretty young girl, the object of his vague sexual fantasy, she is acquainted with a famous writer friend of her father's, whom the envious Marcel dreams of meeting. Thus, like Swann himself, she also incarnates the themes of love and art.

Prior to falling in love with Gilberte, however, the boy has another dream romance. Alone in his room, he spends hours with a magic lantern* and is especially fascinated by one colorful medieval tableau in which a cavalier is pursuing a maiden named Geneviève de Brabant. This spellbinding image, though chronologically distant, is closely related to the present Combray, for one of Geneviève's descendants is that very Duchesse de Guermantes whose mysterious "castle" lies beyond the limit of the family's promenades.

Just as Swann's name seems "almost mythological" to him, so it is with the magical name Guermantes. He builds fantasies around the Duchesse, develops an infatuation, and then one morning in church he sees her. One might expect a romantic analogy between stained-glass windows and magic-lantern projections. On the contrary, we witness the first of Marcel's coldly disappointing discoveries of the breach between subjective illusion and objective reality. He sees a plain-looking, very red-faced woman with a pimple on her nose; except for the elegance of her attire, she could be a shopkeeper's wife. The boy makes an instinctive effort to salvage his illusion. Recalling that she is, after all, the noble descendant of an illustrious family, he reimposes upon this ordinary human being the fairy-tale quality needed to maintain his dream. In this refurbished fantasy, he nurtures the idea that she will return his admiring love, invite him to go fishing, and discuss with him the poems he is writing.

The Combray episode lies outside chronology. It is not a single spring or summer, but a *fusion* of memories—boredom and enchantment, love and loneliness, a quickening intellect, awakening sensuality. It is the time of a boy's dreams.

The World of Balbec. In keeping with Proust's technique of leisurely narrative, simulating the undisciplined

---

* A magic lantern was an optical instrument for projecting magnified pictures on a screen or wall. Also called a stereopticon, it was a precursor of today's slide projector.

processes of dream and memory, the name Balbec appears sporadically throughout the first volume. In the second, like all Combray springing out of a teacup, this seaside resort of the Norman-Breton coast bursts forth with the sun-filled blaze of white beaches, the strange smell of salt air, the kaleidoscope of sea, sky, and young girls in their brightly colored summer outfits. In contrast to Combray, it is a world of fluidity and movement.

The charming English title of Proust's second volume, *Within a Budding Grove,* nonetheless falls short of the original, *A l'ombre des jeunes filles en fleur,* which literally means "in the shadow of young girls in blossom." If we consider Proust's novel as a chronological pilgrimage, this is the "adolescent" volume. Thus the word *shadow* (missing in translation) invokes the boy's feeling of isolation as a stranger to this vacation community where young people all know each other and enjoy a communal social life. Like Gilberte's world or that of the Duchesse, it is one from which he is excluded.

The young Narrator has come to Balbec, in the company of his grandmother and the family servant Françoise, partly because of his health, as a kind of rest cure. The trip further represents the fulfillment of several dreams. He has heard and read of wild storms and shipwrecks along these shores; having formed of them a mental picture, he longs to behold the reality. Swann has also described for him the architecture of the ancient church of Balbec, which the boy indiscriminately includes in his dream picture of the stormy coastline. He first discovers that the church stands several miles inland, not overlooking the sea at Balbec Beach. In addition, it fails in any way to correspond to the church of his imagination. This double disappointment is symptomatic of Proust's constant concern with the encounter between dream and reality, and the inevitable inadequacy of the lat-

ter to fulfill the demands of that "reality" that we have
created in our minds.

Had he thought more realistically, Marcel would have
realized that his mental image of a Balbec dashed by angry
waves was hardly what he would find at the height of summer. What he witnesses instead is the elegant panorama of
wealthy vacationers, suffused in misty sunlight, not unlike
an impressionist painting of the period. As these costumed
figures parade mechanically through round-the-clock rituals
at the Grand Hotel, they do exercise a kind of fascination
for him. Yet their magic is not unmixed with disappointment, for it is not what he had expected, and a difficult
adjustment must be made before he can acclimate to the
"true" Balbec.

This is further dramatized by the difficulty he experiences in adjusting to the strangeness of his hotel room, for
the Narrator depicts himself as a youth of delicate physical
constitution and gravely heightened nervous sensibility.
Eager for adventure, he is nonetheless ill equipped to cope
with the discomforts of change. Unable to sustain the shock
of an unfamiliar reality, he retreats to his bed (not unlike
Aunt Léonie) and into the world of sleep. Just as the first
volume focuses on rooms and dreams, illusion and reality,
the second carries forth these themes.

Still another illusion accompanies Marcel, the disturbing adolescent desire for female companionship. Like most
boys, he has heard from his friends how easy it is to "make
a conquest," but to him all girls seem inaccessible. He
continually nurtures the reverie that he may, in some mysterious fashion, become part of another's existence, physically and spiritually necessary to her being. As with his
          of a beach, a church, a Duchesse, he is once more
courting disillusion.

On several occasions, his eyes meet those of a young
waitress or milkmaid, but it is only in passing, and circum-

stances prevent his determining whether or not she might have been "accessible." During one solitary promenade, however, he is fascinated by a group of tanned, athletic adolescent girls and instantly determines he will get to know them and become part of their world. At first, like Frankie in Carson McCullers's *Member of the Wedding,* he senses only an indefinable desire to be "part of them." They seem to represent that collective femininity heretofore unattainable. Gradually, as he intently observes their frivolous horseplay, he begins to distinguish each girl as an individual and a possible object of his desires.

This section of *Within a Budding Grove,* which bears no title in French, is appropriately called "Seascape with Frieze of Girls" by the English translator. Indeed, Marcel initially perceives them as a total tableau, likening them to a Grecian statuary grouping. Like an artist sketching, he mentally records his perceptions at two levels, simultaneously conceiving the group as a whole yet delineating each girl separately. It is by no aesthetic coincidence that Proust arranges for his young Narrator to meet these girls through the good graces of a painter who has his studio at Balbec and who is a friend of Swann, the boy's artistic mentor.

One girl in particular commands his attention, not because she is more or less attractive than the others, but because an inexplicable quality within her seems to reach out to him. So it is from his initial vision of this rather simple girl, Albertine—wearing a polo cap pulled down around her ears and wheeling a bicycle—that he becomes obsessed with the desire to possess. His attempt, in later volumes, to make of her his exclusive "prisoner" is destined to end with the Narrator himself once more the prisoner, enslaved by a passion over which he has no control. By the end of the Balbec sequence, he has achieved what seems the realization of a cherished fantasy: they are alone in her room. But even so, he is refused even the most chaste of kisses, this refusal firing him on to a still more maddening desire to attain the unattainable. The scene ends with a protesting Albertine ringing the service bell, an echo of that bell which, at Combray, announced Swann's arrival and the deprivation of his mother's kiss.

Meanwhile, during the Balbec stay—such is Proust's mastery of parallel structure—Marcel's pursuit of another impossible ideal, the Duchesse de Guermantes, is being advanced in ways of which he is unaware. A chance encounter with the Marquise de Villeparisis, a childhood friend of his grandmother's, leads to a series of acquaintances that will open the doors to the world of the Guermantes. For the Marquise (although Marcel's grandmother, unaffected by caste consciousness, was not keenly aware of it) is herself a Guermantes!

Proust's point, once we have seen beyond the superficial facade of fictional chance encounter, is this: while we nurture idealistic dreams and suffer from their disillusioning collision with reality, a pattern of life forces is at work, unbeknown to us, bringing us closer to the objects of our reveries. It is our blindness to the pattern of our existence, our involvement with the obvious and concrete, that inhibit our recognition of revelations. In Marcel's eyes, the Marquise is a gracious if somewhat affected old lady who went to school with his grandmother. He could not conceive that she might be related to a far-off goddess, the Duchesse de Guermantes, who embodies for him medieval pageantry, centuries of royal history, legends of a near-mythological age, and a mysterious path never traveled at Combray. The Marquise de Villeparisis exists only in the present, the Duchesse in a distant past and future. But the woman who invites the young Narrator to tea and for carriage rides, is, in point of fact, the Duchesse de Guermantes's own aunt. There is magic and wonderment in our everyday lives, all about us when we least realize it, and when our senses are least open to its discovery.

On one hand, the band of budding girls seems an impenetrable fortress; suddenly, by unexpected chance, he is welcomed into their circle, only to find that attainment is not total attainment when he is rebuffed by Albertine. Meanwhile, the friendship of the Marquise, essentially a matter of indifference to him, is the true talisman to that coveted and fabled world of Guermantes. Near the beach one day, the Narrator spies an elegant, godlike young dandy, the Marquis de St. Loup, and is struck by his aloof and aristocratic demeanor. Is it possible, he wonders, that this divinity from another world might take note of him, might assuage a little that lonely adolescent longing for friendship? In another Balbec incident, the Narrator is in turn observed by a splendidly attired gentleman whose odd actions suggest he may be a spy or a thief who preys on wealthy vacationers. In the Proustian universe, as we have seen, the dream on which we so intensely focus is subject to disillusion, while miracles, when we least attend them, are often casually at hand. Both the majestic Robert de St. Loup and that mysterious stranger, the Baron de Charlus, are also members of the Guermantes family, and as kinsmen of the Marquise, become an unexpected part of Marcel's widening adolescent world and his pursuit of the Duchesse.

The World of the Guermantes.   The reader now begins to see, though the Narrator himself does not, that the events of Balbec have their roots in Combray. It was M. Swann who suggested his going to Balbec; it is his grandmother who knows one of the "lesser" Guermantes vacationing there, the Marquise de Villeparisis. In this widening of his worlds, the Narrator has taken "Swann's way" and found himself en route to the coveted "Guermantes way."

Through the evolution of a complex, invisible pattern, he has gained access to three generations of Guermantes. Robert, the Marquis de St. Loup, becomes a career army officer and will move only sporadically in and out of the Narrator's life. Nor does the Marquise play a sustained major role in the novel, yet it is she who provides the Narrator's introduction into society by inviting him to her Parisian salon. This, in turn, infuriates her nephew, the Baron de Charlus, who portrays himself as the supreme arbiter of the Faubourg, without whose approval no one is admitted to its inner sanctum. Marcel, who finds this pompous gentleman perplexing and intriguing (not yet knowing that he is the Duc de Guermantes's brother), has inadvertently called the Baron's bluff!

At the heart of this ironic incident lies the beginning of a masterful portrait: the Baron de Charlus, destined to become one of Proust's most forceful characters. It is ironic, too, that when the Narrator's parents take a new apartment in Paris, they find themselves neighbors to the Duc and Duchesse de Guermantes. A measure of accessibility, not possible in provincial Combray, is suddenly at hand. Yet the passage of time and growing familiarity lead to the boy's inevitable disenchantment with his dream Duchesse. Girls his own age come to radiate more immediate attractions; seeing Mme. de Guermantes daily also serves to erode her romantic aura. Most of all, there is an even harsher confrontation with reality. Despite her elegance, her position, and the magic of her name, the rather common-looking lady in the Combray church proves in fact to be quite common.

Beneath her historical and cosmetic veneer, the Narrator discovers a rather cruel, crass woman. Noted for epitomizing "the Guermantes wit," she is perhaps less clever than vicious, for her brittle, surface humor frequently involves the devastation of others. The Duc is less haughty, but his bumbling affectations of equality are grounded in innate snobbery. He makes a characteristic show of helping people on with their coats, which prompts the Narrator to recall that a traditional function of the nobility was to attend the king. In so doing, the Duc de Guermantes hopes to be accepted as an unassuming "good fellow." The embarrassing effect is quite opposite.

The Narrator's rise in the social hierarchy follows a prescribed protocol. From the salon of the Marquise, who, with casual pretension, sits painting flowers while her guests mill about, he moves upward to dinner with the Duc and Duchesse. He learns that the Marquise no longer occupies a very privileged place in Faubourg hierarchy, that her mighty niece, the Duchesse, actually is only helping her save face by appearing at her parties, thus contributing to their success. And while the Duchesse is the reigning "queen" of the Faubourg, the greatest *official* honor is to be received by her cousin, the Princesse de Guermantes.

There is, in *Remembrance of Things Past,* a cycle of five great social events attended by the Narrator. These, like his fused memories of Combray, are intended to recapture the essential of presumably countless forays into Parisian society. Observing and listening with him, we come to sense the monotony and the shallowness, to detect the drabness of a tarnishing glitter. The drama of the Narrator's ultimate disillusion, of which his disenchantment with the Duchesse is a harbinger, may best be brought into focus by contrasting the first and the last of the brilliant social gatherings that he records. The first is a spectacular soirée at the Opéra where every notable of the aristocratic social register is to be seen, together with the attendant *arrivistes,* whose chief aim in life is to achieve some measure of participation in the fabled existence of families like the Guermantes. To be invited to such an outing or to a salon of the Faubourg St. Germain was to be blessed by the gods.

It is as gods that they appear to the Narrator, displayed

in the full glory of costumed splendor—a theatrical event to match Marcel's imagination and the kaleidoscopic panorama of his magic lantern. He has previously noted that his mythological Guermantes have a common characteristic, their "family nose" resembling a bird's beak. He sees them bedecked in "plumage." In a conscious shift of metaphor, the audience at the Opéra are described as nymphs and fishes, marine creatures, gods and goddesses of rivers, lakes, and oceans; the Opéra is transformed into a majestic aquarium. The comic effect is heightened by a play on words wherein *baignoire* (loge or mezzanine) also means bathtub. In reflecting on the Duchesse, the Narrator recalls that an enchanted aquatic deity, Mélusine, watched over the fate of that medieval house from which the House of Guermantes descends. Should she vanish, so too would the race. Herein lies an early clue that the Guermantes, like Marcel's illusions, are destined to fade.

This masterful episode, where legend and social satire precariously commingle, is a model of Proustian perspective as a novelistic technique. We sense simultaneously the bewitchment of the young Marcel and the more subtly detached irony of the mature Narrator. This dual point of view, as the past is recaptured in a living present, prevails until the final volume.

Years have passed; the Narrator goes to a Guermantes *matinée* attended by the same eternal socialites, but they are now virtually extinct—physically decrepit and socially impotent, having been seemingly swallowed up, as fish devour their fellows, by the avaricious nouveau riche, those social climbers they once grudgingly tolerated but privately disdained. It is this great illuminating scene that enables the Narrator, retrospectively, to reconstruct the worlds he has known and evaluate what meaning, if any, they retain now that time has dimmed their luster.

Throughout *Remembrance of Things Past,* snobbery in

diverse forms is one of the many vices brought to light. Turn-of-the-century Paris is seen as a maelstrom of burning ambition, a battleground of "ins" and "outs." A minor personage, Mme. de Saint-Euverte, calculates the number of years it will take to establish social eminence. Maneuvering invitations, she uses them to meet the "right" people and in turn invite them as a way of building her own salon. Mme. Verdurin, a more dominant character and the epitome of reverse snobbery, affects indifference to rank and title. While veritably lusting to receive the nobility, she achieves a reputation as hostess of a "little clan" where an atmosphere of unpretentious camaraderie is encouraged. The novel shifts between the Guermantes world and the ascendant realm of the bourgeois Verdurins. Stripped of superficial traits, these worlds are one, as is demonstrated in parallel episodes.

As the Duc and Duchesse de Guermantes are about to leave for dinner and a masquerade ball, word comes that a cousin is dying—an untenable disruption of their evening. The Duc dismisses it as rumor and exaggeration. Accompanying them to their carriage, their good friend Swann discloses that he himself is fatally ill. This too is glossed over by the couple, impatient to begin their evening's amusement. The Duc's offhand remark that he is "dying of hunger" and his fear that his wife will arrive at dinner "dead tired" add bite to their callous indifference.

Yet when the Duc notices that the Duchesse is wearing black shoes with her red gown, this takes precedence over all. While there was no time for commiseration, there is time to find the "correct" pair of red shoes. Symbolically, the Guermantes repudiate death and its color of mourning, clinging to the red blood of life.

This celebrated episode should not be interpreted, however, solely as an indictment of the aristocratic temperament, for the identical ritual is performed by the bourgeois Verdurins. On two occasions, news of death threatens to spoil their entertainment and is similarly dismissed by being banished from the conversation. In the world of society, at whatever level, values become distorted, with pleasure and propriety transcending pity and human allegiance. Man recklessly plays god by daring to defy death; he insists on having his party.

The World of Sodom and Gomorrah. The symbolic "cities of the plain" in volume four of *Remembrance of Things Past* are the Sodom and Gomorrah of Biblical legend, damned for the immorality of sexual inversion. While Proust was not the first French novelist to approach homosexuality as a theme, nowhere had the subject been treated so openly and extensively.

Many early readers were disturbed by a scene in *Swann's Way* in which the music teacher's daughter at Combray, Mlle. Vinteuil, is seen indulging in lesbian embraces. She taunts her companion with the idea that the photograph of her dead father may be "watching" them, whereupon the other girl spits on the picture. The episode seemed not only unsavory, but gratuitously so. In effect, Proust was announcing a theme that emerges hundreds of pages later, with great drama and significance. The act itself is even expiated in the final volume when the memory of M. Vinteuil is honored.

The curious behavior of the Baron de Charlus becomes at last understandable when the ostentatiously virile Baron is discovered to be homosexual. The young Narrator does not at first comprehend aspects of this world, nor does the reader. Proust's method throughout is one of progressive revelation, and every element of the novel is designed to form part of a total structure: the random, remembered experiences of the Narrator made intelligible as a coherent whole. Because he has idolized the historically noble Guermantes family, the discovery of homosexuality in that lineage becomes another disillusion, a symbol of their weakness and degeneration. The colorful paradise he imagines and the shadow of sexual inversion that haunts the Faubourg St. Germain provide a forceful contrast.

Thus, to the worlds of Combray, Balbec, and Parisian society, Proust affixed an "underworld" of the damned. In the Narrator's eyes, the many inverts—thought by some critics to be too numerous in the book—represent a closed secret society. He is interested in their need to wear masks. In the case of a socially prominent noble like Charlus, it becomes the second mask of a man moving simultaneously in two worlds, playing two roles, both false.

Homosexuality is seen as a leveler that transcends artificial spheres, cutting across class, uniting princes and servants in an uneasy alliance. In one Guermantes episode, a young nobleman is about to be announced by a footman when each recognizes the other as his partner in a recent chance homosexual encounter. At that time, neither knew the other's identity nor revealed his own. Proust, while recording the thoughts and emotions of each, freezes them in a brief moment of time, an impossible moment of truth. They are cast in a stylized tableau of that prison-like society in which they are opposites but equals, lovers but enemies, each holding a respective rank but both essentially outcasts.

More psychologist than sociologist, Proust was also deeply interested in the personal manias that grip our lives and control our actions, often to the point of obsession. Mme. Verdurin relentlessly pursues social success; the Baron de Charlus becomes a slave to what Proust calls his "vice." The Narrator's own behavior is dominated by an idealistic penchant for illusion that leads to a dangerous disequilibrium in his life. In his pursuit of dreams and the unknown, his desire to possess the impossible, he finds himself, as we shall see, a reluctant and bewildered intruder in the alien world of Sodom and Gomorrah.

There is also the world of art. Since Swann and the
Baron de Charlus are knowledgeable in literature, painting,
and music, the novel abounds in artistic references and aesthetic theory. The Narrator also meets an author and a
painter, and the impact of these encounters will leave its
mark on his life and his view of life. A musical theme
ultimately helps give dimension to his self-understanding.
From boyhood, he entertains that restless dream of becoming a writer. In his partly chivalric, partly sensual fantasies,
he imagines himself telling the Duchesse about a novel he
will write. The essence of that dream never leaves him, and
periodically, all during his life, he laments not having had
the powers of insight and observation necessary to a writer.
He also decries time lost in the pursuit of idle illusions such
as social vanity and essentially unobtainable love.

In the first few pages of *Remembrance of Things Past,*
the Narrator conveys in a single sentence the quintessence of
his early years. In the only room of Aunt Léonie's house
that is ever locked, he finds a refuge, the necessary isolation to indulge himself in the solitary pastimes of "reading,
reverie, tears and sensuality." It is a revealing equation in
which art, dreams, sorrow, and the pleasures of solitary sex
are interrelated in a composite figure that symbolizes not
only a childhood, but a life and the novel of that life.

The Narrator's recollections form a "book of worlds."
Combray and Balbec are spatial worlds corresponding to the
temporal worlds of childhood and adolescence. Even though
much of the novel takes place in Paris, there is no "world of
Paris" as such. It is there as a vivid presence, in the Narrator's
memory and in the novel, yet Gilberte in Paris is still part of
his Combray world and Albertine in Paris remains part of
his Balbec world. The Guermantes world exists on two
planes: as a social phenomenon with the spatial shape of the
Faubourg St. Germain and, through the Duchesse, as a timeless world of poetry and legend. The name Guermantes

permeates both Combray and Balbec, just as the symbolic world of Sodom and Gomorrah is in turn related to all the others.

His adult world has no tangible locus in either time or space. Throughout the novel, we find ourselves in the extra-temporal universe of the Narrator's memory. He exists for the most part within the shifting boundaries of his own mental worlds. There, illusion and reality are at times happily indistinguishable; sorrow comes when they clash. It is the alternation of these two emotional states that produces the tension of Proust's novel. And when the various worlds of *Remembrance of Things Past* are ultimately superimposed and memorialized through imagination and art, that tension is resolved. All may be seen as facets of a single world, a world of dreams projected, illusion and disillusion alike recaptured in memory—a magic-lantern world.

2

Prisoners of Illusion

The mad, sad desire to possess
—*M.P.*

Remembrance of Things Past was published over a long period: *Swann's Way* in 1913 and the final volume, *The Past Recaptured*, not until 1927, five years after Proust's death. By the time the first few volumes had appeared, he was both widely praised and damned for creating such "microscopic" studies of human character. To these contradictory critiques, he replied: ". . . for I had been using, on the contrary, a telescope, in order to perceive things, often minute because of their great distance, yet each a world unto itself. Where I had been searching out great laws, they said I was combing for details."

What are those "great laws?" Proust, as we have seen, sought to deal with time and memory in a unique way; he sometimes even capitalized these terms as though they were dramatic personages, not abstract phenomena. The incident of the *madeleine* dipped in tea is a dramatic example of *mémoire involontaire,* the sudden, spontaneous outrush of recollections, once more tangibly present though we thought them buried and forgotten. Quite independently of Freud, Proust perceived the human mind as a great storehouse of memories, accessible to us under exceptional and fortuitous circumstances that he calls "privileged." It is not through voluntary memory—a conscious effort to recapture the past —but rather through the free, accidental play of sensory associations that we cut across time, reactivate and virtually relive certain moments that had seemed irretrievably lost.

Proust recognized time for precisely what it is: an artificial creation designed by man to measure and to structure experience. Recognizing temporal limitations and the way in which we become slaves to the artifice, he developed the concept of subjective human time: our experiences as they relate to one another, irrespective of chronology. In such a scheme, past, present, and future are reduced to a common plane, each individual's perception of the world. So it is with our perception of people, as well. Proust both demonstrates

28

and discusses human existence in terms of "successive selves." From the start of the novel, Marcel observes not one person but a multiplicity of personages in M. Swann. This does not merely mean that the character is complex or that he is acting out "roles" (although these, of course, are possibilities). The Proustian succession of selves represents the various stages at which we progressively know a person and the nature of our relationship at a given period of time— even a given moment—for he perceived human personality as being in a state of continual flux.

Swann's origins, like those of the Narrator, are middle class. But he has risen in the social ranks and is on close terms with members of the nobility. At Combray, however, where bourgeois notions of caste prevail, the Narrator's family sees him only as "young Swann," son of the elder Swann, an old family friend. This is how they are accustomed to view him, and any indication of his ties with the aristocracy are received with laughter or disbelief. (In just the same way, as we have seen, the Narrator's grandmother has the Marquise "typed" as an old childhood acquaintance rather than a Guermantes.)

The Narrator remembers Swann in other perspectives. In his eyes, there is Swann the unwelcome visitor whose presence means banishment to his room. But a metamorphosis occurs. Swann becomes the welcome visitor with stories and pictures of far-off places like Venice and Balbec. Then he emerges as the Husband of Odette. When the Narrator falls in love with their daughter, Swann becomes for him the Father of Gilberte. In still another role, he is also a Friend of the Guermantes. It is less the individual than the perception of the Narrator that changes. This theory of successive selves poses the dichotomy of objective and subjective reality, with Proust opting for the latter as the more valid and fertile truth. Reality is in the eyes of the beholder.

Odette and Gilberte are also subject to metamorphosis.

Swann's wife, in fact, provides a wealth of successive selves. She is first mentioned as a scandalous woman whom Swann cannot present to any level of society. As the narrative progresses, both forward and backward in time, the Narrator realizes that Odette had once been his uncle's mistress, a perfumed Lady in Pink to whom he was introduced as a child, thereby causing a great stir in the family. We also have glimpses of her as an artist's model (and perhaps his mistress, too). But such identities are eclipsed when she emerges as the Mother of Gilberte. In loving Gilberte, he transforms both Swann and Odette into ancillary figures. In Proust's view, existence of other people is an inconstant phenomenon, subject both to external change and to our individual, highly subjective perceptions. It is a question of both actuality and illusion. When the widowed Odette remarries, she assumes a new name and a new guise; these are objective transformations to be added to the Narrator's essentially subjective composite of Odette de Crécy Swann de Forcheville.

The Duchesse de Guermantes, as we have seen, also undergoes a metamorphosis. The reality, looking like any other woman in the flesh, fails to coincide with Marcel's illusory Duchesse; it is only through a renewed effort of the imagination that he rekindles his bright illusion. But as she increasingly reveals herself as coarse, common, and selfish, eventually nothing remains for him but her titled name. And this is the "reality" he first fell in love with! If our dreams and illusions pass through a succession of stages, it is also partly because we do so ourselves. Thus the Narrator progressively sees himself as "the me that loved the Duchesse" or "the me that once loved Gilberte." It is the vain quest for a constant, permanent identity that he is pursuing.

Related to the problems of time, memory, and identity is the problem of emotional discontinuity, what Proust calls "intermittences of the heart." When the Narrator returns to

Balbec for a second visit, he is no longer an adolescent but a young man, and he has lost his grandmother of whom he was extremely fond. Amidst his *conscious* recollections of the earlier trip, a sudden, unexpected memory of her leaps even more vividly to the fore. As he bends to unbutton his boots, the physical sensations of that movement reproduce not only a prior experience but the emotional content of that experience.

Weary and despondent, as he was on arriving at Balbec the first time, he abruptly senses with intensity the physical and spiritual presence of the grandmother who consoled him then. In the interim, despite his love, he has not truly felt the impact of her death. For the first time, he knows the anguish of that loss. Her absence becomes a real and haunting presence.

So it is that our various memories of a person, a place, or an event lie dormant within us. We live in a continual state of emotional vacillation, subject to the sporadic return of feelings we had once felt and, equally, to their sudden unaccountable disappearance. The "me" who once existed, harboring certain states of mind and sentiments is not irreparably washed away by time but may resurge intact when least expected through the medium of involuntary memory. All of our former selves are potentially part of our present, however past and buried they may seem:

It is quite probably the presence of our body, seeming to us like a vase enveloping our spiritual side, that leads us to suppose that all our inner possessions, our past joys and sorrows, are a perpetual part of us. While it is perhaps untrue to say they depart and return, if they do remain within us it is for the most part in some unknown realm where they are of no avail to us . . . but if the structure of sensations that houses them is once reached again, they have the force to drive out all that is alien to them and to restore exclusively that self who once lived those experiences and emotions.

This is perhaps the most significant thesis in the Proustian process of self-discovery, one of the "great laws" governing existence, and accounting in great measure for the inconsistencies and contradictions of character within us. One's whole being—self in its totality—is perceived incompletely if we accept only the time-ordered succession of selves and fail to acknowledge the coherent synthesis of selves existing simultaneously in the mind.

Another demon for Proust, along with time, is habit. Woven among the Narrator's memories of Combray, there is a philosophic thread on the psychology of habit, which he sees as an anesthetic. Despite the carefree mood of spring vacation, Marcel senses the bare rigidity with which members of the household act out their daily existence in perfunctory, mechanical patterns. At the same time, there is comfort in the routine and the expected; they shield us from the shock of novelty and the need to respond to life in unwonted ways. Family meals, discussions of the weather, country walks, Swann's visits, are all safely determined events whose continuity no one would alter—except Marcel perhaps, but he too is largely an unventuresome creature of habit. Much of the escapist romance in his life originates in the projections of his magic lantern, but even the pleasures of that fantastic extratemporal world pose a dilemma: "Yet my unhappiness was deepened as a result of the magic lantern, since the very alteration in lighting disrupted my habitual perception of my room, which, save for the torture of having to go to bed, had become bearable only out of sheer habit."

His visit to Balbec Beach is an occasion for dreams and anticipation, yet the boy suffers a kind of terror at the prospect of new and unfamiliar surroundings. He is too old to be scared in a conventional childish way, but his sensitivity is such that any disruption of accepted patterns seems a menace. Once we have come to grips with the unknown and made it part of us, Proust indicates, the frighteningly new and adventurous becomes in turn the comfortably familiar. Habit has set in. While Proust envisions the habitual, in psychological terms, as a source of solace, he sees it also as a process of stultification. It becomes a sheltering wall but one that inhibits our capacity for seeing beyond the immediate, from living life to the fullest measure of its promise. Thus, we may come to "live with" anything, but if time comforts and conditions, through habit it also dulls our perceptions and our feelings. Such deadening is a kind of dying.

Demonstrations of these Proustian "laws," as well as theoretical elaborations, run heavily throughout the novel. What Proust means by "the succession of selves" and "intermittences of the heart" becomes particularly apparent within the framework of Proust's psychology of love. Over the years, the Narrator describes various romantic liaisons, which, though different in their superficial aspects, are essentially variations on a single theme: love's impossibility.

Marcel's infatuation with Gilberte Swann is destined to follow the same course as his abortive love for the Duchesse. The adolescent affair with Albertine fades, then flares again when they are somewhat older. It continues to fade and flare intermittently, achieving a particular intensity as her "mystery" and inaccessibility grow more tantalizing. At the same time, the Narrator progressively grasps the true character of the Baron de Charlus and comes to understand the Baron's relationship with a young musician. A homosexual affair, he observes, follows basically the same pattern as any other. But the prototype of all the love affairs in the novel, and chronologically the first, is Swann's liaison with Odette.

Swann in Love, which constitutes a substantial portion of the first volume, is a perfect novella in itself. It can be read, and frequently is read, independently. This is also the only section of the novel that is not told in the first person, since the events took place prior to the Narrator's birth. The flashback device also enables the author to introduce the bourgeois Verdurin group, which serves as a foil to the aristocratic world of the Guermantes. For it is under the wing of Mme. Verdurin that the affair flourishes. This is not a milieu that Swann would frequent of his own volition, but since it is Odette's world, it is there that he must be.

When he first met Odette, casually at the theater, Swann had been indifferent to her. Though she has a certain chic and charm, greatly admired by both sexes, hers is not the type of beauty to which he is drawn. On the one hand, Swann is accustomed to the more authentic stylishness of Parisian noblewomen; on the other, he has a perverse taste for clandestine affairs with chambermaids and waitresses. Odette de Crécy, *cocotte* and *demimondaine,* belongs to neither of these familiar worlds, and so his instinctive reaction is one of rejection.

It is Odette who makes the first advances. An accomplished coquette, she flatters Swann on the range of his artistic knowledge and pursuits, coyly expressing her eagerness to learn from him. Their meetings multiply and, almost imperceptibly, a liaison ensues. There is nothing sentimental or conventionally romantic about their relationship; it is chiefly through acquiring the *habit* of Odette that Swann comes to love Odette to the point where he cannot live without her. He becomes, almost nightly, a regular guest at the Verdurins.

By way of contrast to the formalities of the Faubourg St. Germain, Mme. Verdurin self-consciously affects the absence of affectation as the standard of her soirées. She cultivates a down-to-earth atmosphere—no airs or fuss, just "chums" getting together for a good time. In reality, Mme. Verdurin's "clan" members are as rigidly ritualistic as the aristocrats whom she jealously labels "bores." Proust uses the words "credo" and "orthodoxy" to describe the code to which the "faithful" must subscribe. They must not only abjure all contact with "bores," they must appear regularly at her table where their place is permanently reserved, and they must indulge her pretense of suffering during the evening's music. Affecting a hypersensitivity to the emotional impact of art, Mme. Verdurin "gets headaches from Wagner."

Through Swann's eyes, we readily see the Verdurin clique as pretentious bores themselves. The pseudo-intellectual "faithful" include a professor who makes unintelligible puns rooted in esoteric scholarship, a jolly doctor who speaks in clichés, and assorted aspiring artists. They are Dickensian caricatures. Their taste, like Odette's, is essentially vulgar, their vague notions of sophistication are nouveau riche. As Swann's infatuation grows, however, he ceases to see them as they are.

Very early in their affair, Odette vows to be ever at Swann's call, always available to him. At that moment, he does not particularly want her to be so much a part of his life. As time progresses, it is precisely her inaccessibility, the betrayal of her promise, that drives him to desire her more and more: "And it was just such moments when she had forgotten even Swann's very existence that proved more useful to Odette, more instrumental in attaching Swann to her, than all her coquettish ways."

There is a French proverb-play that cautions: one does not play games with love. Swann dares to, and while the result is not death, as in Musset's bittersweet drama, he manages to create the situation he least desired, actually falling in love with Odette. Implementing a coy scheme of his own, Swann has purposely arranged to arrive late one night to call for Odette at the Verdurins, certain that his absence will intensify her desire for him; the ruse boomerangs, however, for she leaves without waiting for him. It is now he whose desires become intensified, and in a scene of desperate pursuit, we follow Swann's carriage along the

boulevards of Paris, stopping at every café in search of
Odette. As the cafés, one by one, lower their lights, he is left
alone, a frantic figure in the empty dark of night. Then,
contrary to his genuine expectations—"He had chased all
over Paris not because he really believed in any chance of
finding her, but because the thought of giving up the search
was too cruel for him"—he finds her. It is on that very night
that she becomes his mistress.

Yet Proust now numbers Swann among the damned.
He has fallen victim to the most grievous and absurd of
human anxieties "which the laws of this world render impossible to satisfy and difficult to remedy—the hapless and in-
sane desire of possession. . . ." In a comparable episode, on
still another night, Swann leaves Odette's apartment but
suffers a premonition that she may be cheating on him and
returns to find a light still in her street floor window, seeming to confirm that she might be entertaining another man.
It is a Molièresque comedy of errors, set in the grotesque
shadows of a Kafka nightmare. Swann raps, waits, and as
the shutters open on an unfamiliar room, discovers that in
his anxiety, he has picked the wrong apartment.

Already the blind, unthinking slave of habit and routine, he now becomes a slave to suspicion and jealousy.
Proust does not differentiate between founded and un-
founded doubts; both are equally destructive, and it is not
their truth that matters but their capacity to devastate. The
debonair, indifferent Swann takes to opening Odette's mail,
spying on her, and staging scenes of Inquisition-like ques-
tioning. Rumors of her infidelity drive him to pursue truths
he can never know with any real certainty. As Proust points
out, with candid pessimism: "Knowing does not always en-
able us to take precautions, yet on learning things we hold
them, perhaps not in our hands, but in our minds . . . which
gives us the illusion that we hold some sway over events."

In seeking to convince himself that his mistress would

not lie, Swann recalls that early in their affair she had openly offered to fib to Mme. Verdurin in order to spend an evening alone with him. Espousing carefully contrived logic, he seeks to determine her *pattern* of lies; it is just his misfortune that Odette's spontaneous responses are a random set of falsehoods, truths and half-truths, defying coherence. One rumor he hears would impute lesbian activities to Odette. Her outright denial yields to a disquieting "maybe two or three times," and finally to an avowal that totally routs the direction of his inquiry. Swann had assumed that such experiences, if any, would somehow belong to a distant past; he learns instead of one instance so recent it must necessarily have taken place since he has known her. But is she telling the truth or ingenuously fabricating? He cannot be sure. He cannot know Odette, can never possess her, past, present or future; she cannot be *his,* which is, in spite of all, what he must have.

Odette, a not very intelligent *cocotte* for whom he initially felt indifference, has become a chimera to whose pursuit he is now inexorably bound. One stage in the progress of his infatuation was when he discovered her resemblance to a Botticelli painting. Art is a constant frame of reference for Swann, who best interprets reality through esthetic correlations. On looking at a reproduction of the Botticelli, he is better able to conjure Odette than on looking at her photograph. While this may be taken as a cross-reference to one of Proust's major themes, the interplay of art and reality, it is even more pointedly his demonstration of a psychological tenet: we do not "love" another being but rather, from desire and imagination, subjectively fashion a creation that will correspond to our dream.

Swann's happiest hours, his only true hours of calm, are those spent in purely subjective projections of Odette, unimpeded by her physical presence. Yet while meditating on her charms or aspects of her appearance, he recalls that she attracts, has attracted, and will attract other men, other women. Efforts to dispel her from his thoughts only act perversely to reinforce her there, where jealousy and the mania of possession are eroding a once clear and independent will. Pygmalion's Galatea assumes the proportions of a Frankenstein monster.

The echo of her promise, "I'll be there whenever you want me," has faded with the reality of her inconstancy. In a moment of lucid insight, the dazed lover becomes frighteningly aware of passage and transition. He sees before him a succession of Odettes and a succession of Swanns; the fact that there exists no permanent *Swann-Odette* taunts him bitterly. Resorting to an inevitable analogy with the arts, Swann thinks of a Bellini painting, the portrait of Mohammed II who became so enamored of his mistress that he had her killed in order to free himself of her enchantment.

It is not in painting, though, nor yet in murder, that he finds the peace of liberation. During one calm, untroubled period of their relationship, Swann had adopted as the symbol of their love the musical theme from a Vinteuil sonata played at Mme. Verdurin's. Toward the end of *Swann in Love,* now plagued by jealous doubts, he hears that theme once more. In a scene comparable to the Narrator's experience on "tasting" his Combray past in a cup of tea, Swann recaptures the happiness of those moments when he and Odette had enjoyed a reciprocal love—or so he believed. In the midst of an uncertain present, that fleeting time returns, contained within the music, and envelops him like an eternal permanence. Yet he suffers from the knowledge that Odette will probably never be his again. On the one hand, he would like to be free, but he cannot bear the anguish of her loss. The reader now senses that Swann is inexorably destined to make her his wife.

He makes what Proust considered a great human error: he has traded the perfection of remembered joy—dead in the realm of time but infinite in the realm of memory—for the futile "possession" of a reality. A prisoner of immutable psychological patterns, Swann has this last ironic, bitter-sweet realization: "To think I've wasted years of my life, that I wanted to die, that I experienced my greatest love, all for a woman I didn't essentially care for, who wasn't my type at all."

The Narrator's love for Gilberte begins with her name, which he endows with an aura of mystery and desire. For him, Swann is the Enchanter, and magicians have princesses for daughters. He imagines with jealous longing the fabled existence she must lead. One spring afternoon, in a soft setting of Combray hawthorns, he sees Gilberte, accompanied by a Lady in White and a Mysterious Gentleman. As their eyes meet, she returns his moonstruck gaze with an enigmatic smile and a gesture so strangely insolent, coming from a young girl, that it inspires contradictory emotions: "I was in love with her, I kept regretting I had not had the time or the inspiration to offend her, to do her harm, to make her remember me."

The magic sound "Gilberte," as her mother calls out to her, echoes in his mind until he hears it again that autumn in Paris. One of her friends is saying goodbye to her, and as the boy watches her leave, he wonders if she will ever again return to that park along the Champs-Elysées. She does, of course, the very next day. They become friends, and so begins a winter of rapture and of torment. The joyous prospect of being with her after school is constantly menaced by the possibility that she may not come that day. Some days he knows in advance that he will not see her, and the certainty of that sorrow is preferable to the anguish of doubt.

In quite the same way that Gilberte's father became enslaved by Odette, the young Narrator lets his whole existence come to be dominated by thoughts of Gilberte. If the Swann/Odette episode is told with clinical detachment, here we sense the warm, newly awakened feelings of an infatuated youth, but also the intensity of his frustrations.

He writes the name "Gilberte Swann" over and over in his notebooks with the almost mystical belief that somehow the words may summon her presence. He writes her letters, some telling her of his affections, some denying them. Some of these he sends, others he destroys; all are an exercise in futility, for in Proust's psychology, we love alone. In every affair, there is the one who loves and the one who is loved. The obsessed young Narrator finds excuses to talk with his parents about Gilberte's family, to discuss their apartment, the building, the street where they live. He makes the fatal error of becoming jealous of the life Gilberte leads when they are not together.

The weather suddenly becomes enormously important to him, for if it is rainy or snowing, there will be no Gilberte that day. The most provocative factor in his love, though, is Gilberte's indifference to him; this, above all, generates his desires to become part of her world. It is partly a reaching out to possess her, but also a striving for identity. The Narrator learns early in life the difficulties that emerge when we are first overtaken by an awareness of ourselves in the eyes of others. How does she see him? How do her parents see him? These are taunting questions. He seeks, by imitation, to identify with Gilberte's sphere of existence. Everything about her world is wondrous, even a little blue feather in the cap of her governess. Why, he wonders, shouldn't Françoise, his own governess, wear a blue feather in her cap?

Then, time and habit begin their work of cyclical erosion. As he is welcomed into Gilberte's home and becomes a regular guest, the distant enchantment of unattainability fades into routine reality. Having exhausted every mental variation of desire, jealousy, and despair within the modest confines of his psychological make-up, he reaches the stage where he is "free" from Gilberte, while Swann, on the contrary, could not liberate himself from Odette. The Narrator's juvenile romance ends where Swann's began: on an emotional plateau of indifference. It is at this point in the narrative that he visits Balbec Beach and chooses Albertine from the group of "young girls in flower." There is little indication in that volume, *Within a Budding Grove,* that the affair will be more than an adolescent summer romance. Returning to Paris, he begins to make his mark in the social world. Although he continues to see Albertine, their relationship is casual; it is overshadowed by his preoccupation with the Faubourg St. Germain, his alternating fascination and disenchantment with its mysteries and inanities. Ever in search of love, the young Narrator also continues to project illusions, concocting ill-fated schemes of seduction and dreaming that some chance encounter will materialize into his ideal of romance.

It is not until part way through *Cities of the Plain* (and so approximately midway through the novel itself) that the Marcel/Albertine affair takes on new definition. From that point, it assumes vast and grim proportions. The agony of unrequited love, already delineated as a key Proustian theme, takes on a nightmare aura as Marcel blindly repeats not only the errors and follies of Swann but those of his own desperate infatuation with Gilberte. In a psychological analysis unprecedented in literature, Proust devoted two full volumes of his seven-volume work (*The Captive* and *The Sweet Cheat Gone*) to the frustrating drama of Marcel and Albertine. The essence of that drama, however, is already clearly evident in the distilled form of a single scene, centering on a telephone call.

The Narrator is nervously awaiting Albertine. His initial annoyance at her lateness yields to mounting anxiety. His mind pursues that masochistic logic which supposes that the object of one's desires is in the company of someone else. The less certain her arrival, the greater his desire—and his torment. When the phone rings, he has correctly anticipated the conversation: the hour being so late, she will probably not meet him after all. He feigns indifference, saying how tired he is. She pleads forgetfulness, asks forgiveness. Both are lying, to themselves and to each other. When Albertine suggests they meet the next day, he risks the incredibly bold bluff that he will be "busy for two or three weeks." Without waiting for her response, he takes an even greater gamble, indicating his "willingness" to see her despite his fatigue, for it is best, as he insists she must agree, not to hang up in mutual anger. Within minutes, Albertine arrives by cab.

This same episode, depending on context and style, could be played as farce or melodrama; Proust achieved a tone of psychological tension that transcends both by far. Recalling Combray and the fierce need for his mother's goodnight kiss, the Narrator once more senses the impossible distance that separates desire and possession. He realizes, too, that momentary satisfaction does not gratify but only intensifies longing and desire. This brief assuagement, this "victory" over Albertine, is only temporary release from the anguish of dependence. Yet the fact that he can analyze with great lucidity the pattern of his emotions does not necessarily give him self-control or free him from delusions.

With a false sense of security that Albertine is "his," he feels a kind of freedom from her and decides to go alone to Balbec once more. Just as he outgrew his infatuation for Gilberte, now it is Albertine who will be exorcised. Returning to the same resort hotel, he feels a powerful sensual anticipation, in which the indifferent images of Albertine and Gilberte play no part. His attitude on finding that Albertine is unexpectedly vacationing there recalls Swann's indifference to Odette at those times when she is "accessible."

Albertine's words "If you want me, I'll come running" provide a fatal echo of the Swann/Odette affair. Then, one night at the Casino, Albertine and a girlfriend are waltzing together. Dr. Cottard, one of the Verdurin circle, makes a chance observation to the Narrator that is destined to change his life: "They must be in ecstasy. Not many people know, but it's in the breast that girls really feel sexual pleasure and theirs are certainly touching, look."

His previous anxiety that Albertine enjoyed an existence apart from and unknown to him not only returns but takes on a terrifying new dimension. Although the effect is not immediate (". . . there are poisons," the Narrator notes, "which take time to act"), the fact that Cottard is a bit of a fool but also a physician adds a maddening ambiguity to his remark. The Narrator, moreover, has a store of mental tableaux on which this new image is readily superimposed; he recalls the story of Odette's alleged lesbian excursions and also his own childhood memory of Mlle. Vinteuil in another woman's embrace.

Until now, his feelings toward Albertine have intermittently vacillated between indifference and desire. The pattern is deterministic, one of cause and effect: Albertine inaccessible is more desirable than Albertine accessible. The loved one's absence, some mystery surrounding her, provokes jealousy, and this in turn triggers the need for possession. Within Proust's rigorous psychological schema, the possibility of Albertine's lesbianism becomes the most provocative of mysteries. The Narrator must know the truth. While he might countenance her sleeping with another man, or accept her past affairs with men, her lesbian life poses an impenetrable barrier between her world and his own.

In a more temperate way, both the Duchesse and Gilberte belonged to alien worlds and this was part of their enchantment. Odette's "other life" exercised powers of attraction over the sophisticated Swann. But the idea of Albertine in the world of Gomorrah supposes an aspect of her existence to which Marcel would remain a total stranger. There she would experience a kind of sensuality from which he is utterly excluded. The Narrator thus perceives a myriad of threats to his possession of Albertine. He becomes increasingly determined not to let her from his sight, and to learn if his suspicions are grounded. During the almost constant days they spend together, motoring around the countryside, he finds himself, almost reluctantly but necessarily, keeping Albertine "a prisoner within his watch." In a rare moment of lucidity, he senses the loss of his own individuality and recognizes the folly of the marriage project he has been formulating. Like Swann with Odette, he is intermittently ready to try to end the affair. It is on learning from Albertine herself that she knows Mlle. Vinteuil and her friend "quite intimately" that a dazed Marcel chooses the only possible path, which is also the one impossible path: "I must marry Albertine."

The Captive opens on a scene that closely parallels the first episode of the novel where the Narrator awakens in a darkened room. In that instance, it was night, and we have, in effect, been accompanying the Narrator in a long reverie of remembrance. Now we reach the threshold of manhood; it is a morning in Paris but the dawn of a nightmare. Through heavily draped windows, symbol of sequestration, lively Parisian street sounds are echoed, dramatizing the distance between Marcel and the world outside. He has persuaded Albertine to come and live with him and can scarcely believe his good fortune: she is actually in his "possession." His desire to possess her and keep her from others is gratified. Yet the peace of mind he feels is not so much joy as "appeasement from suffering."

Proust frequently uses such terminology to describe love, which he clearly considers an ill, virtually an illness. It is as though the Narrator were addicted to a drug, for only

Albertine's embraces provide temporary relief from the prospect of suffering. Her presence, though often boring, has become a necessity. There is no longer the desire of longing for her but the need to be sure that she is safe from the eyes and arms of others. He persuades himself that it is morally right to keep her from the reach of women who might corrupt her, but this is a delusion to justify his obsessive mania. Beyond the romantic illusion wherein we seek to become "one" with another person, Proust cynically equates love with the desire for total possession, which he acknowledges at the same time to be a frustrating impossibility.

Love, in *Remembrance of Things Past*, is never reciprocal. It is not only one-sided, but thoroughly subjective: the loved one exists only as a projection of our dreams and desires, a creation of our own imagination. First seen along the beach, Albertine became the embodiment of the Narrator's adolescent sensuality. He seeks, against the incursions of reality, to maintain that Albertine. Wearing a richly brocaded blue gown (which he has bought for her, perhaps to accentuate her femininity), she reminds him of a goddess of the sea. He remembers not only Balbec, but imagines the wonders of Venice and the Adriatic shore. Because she conjures an era of his life—and despite her rather ordinary qualities—he even comes to see her as a "Goddess of Time."

What were Albertine's motives in becoming the Narrator's mistress? These, like the girl herself and the question of her sexual inversion, remain a mystery. He is charming and intelligent; being well off financially, he gives her lavish gifts. But Proust's strange tale transcends the pedestrian machinery of kept woman-jealous lover scenarios. Since it is told exclusively through the eyes of the Narrator, Albertine must remain a mystery for the reader as well. Indeed, we are less concerned here with her apparent submission than with his progressive enslavement.

His love for Albertine, for all its agonizing and self-inflicted torture, is essentially rooted in a psychology of comfort—the comforts of habit and illusion. Although he would be freer and happier without her, he becomes so accustomed to Albertine's "assuagement" he cannot go without. At the same time, he entertains two contradictory illusions: a mythlike mistress corresponding to no reality, and a real person who may or may not be a lesbian. None of her various "selves" is truly accessible to him.

Just as the boy Marcel was emotionally dependent on a nocturnal kiss, now Albertine's kiss becomes his "daily bread." If the love he felt for the Duchesse was a legend of his own making, so it is with Albertine. And since illusions must be preserved from contact with reality, he does his unreasonable best to guard her from the outside world. They do go out together, but if she goes alone, it is in the company of a hired chauffeur or her friend Andrée, both of whom serve as spies for Marcel! The only peace he finds is in watching Albertine sleep. Yet Albertine sleeping, we realize, is akin to Albertine dead. While the Narrator does not consciously contemplate murder, he does consider the possibility of her death, which might provide his only possible release.

Their relationship progressively reaches the stage of intolerable mutual torture. Whatever she says or does will be regarded by him as false; whatever he says or does will smack of the fanatic inquisitor. Each day becomes a theatrical charade in which they recapitulate the roles they earlier played in that midnight telephone call. Several times, when the Narrator proposes that they part company, he is wretched if she agrees and wretched if she does not. One morning, he at last brings himself to the psychological point where he might feasibly endure the end of their affair: it is then that the servant Françoise announces, "Mlle. Albertine has gone." All strength leaves him; he must have her back. In the midst of his elaborate machinations to regain Albertine, in which he sends his friend Robert de St. Loup in search of her, the Narrator receives a series of three abrupt communications. There is a letter from Albertine expressing her willingness to return, a second confirming the finality of her departure, and a telegram from her aunt announcing Albertine's death in an accident on horseback.

The dynamics of Proustian psychology are even more dramatically demonstrated in the pages that follow than in the long, painstaking analysis of their affair. Although the Narrator is not deeply moved by his loss, at least not in any conventional romantic sense, he is stunned by the intervention of fate and also by the recognition of a terrible truth. He is not free at all. What he felt for Albertine was not love but the passion of possessiveness, the impossible lust of owning her soul. That desire is now more impossible than ever. He must go on living with the mystery of Albertine until she finally dies within him as well. He is at the mercy of time the enemy, time the friend.

He is also at the mercy of habit. Since Marcel's total psychological mechanism has been for so long geared to a single pursuit—the truth about Albertine—he continues like a madman in that pursuit. Even after her death, the inquisition goes on. Friends and strangers are interrogated; the servants at Balbec's Grand Hotel are cross-examined. Now that there is no future, the Narrator relentlessly penetrates Albertine's past. Just as he had learned from her toward the end that she never really knew Mlle. Vinteuil, that it was just said to intrigue him, he now stumbles against a barrier of conflicting "truths": that she was lesbian and that she was not.

Looking back, like Swann, he sees the hollowness of what had seemed high drama, high passion. Once more he holds a handful of dust. Through the eyes of the Narrator and his experience, Proust seems at this point to see man as a slave to habit, a prisoner of illusion, a victim of life's

inconstancy. In an intermittent series, we experience ever-
changing, contradictory emotions. We are faced with a succession of various identities—both our own and those of
others. There is no truth, no permanence, no reality except
that which is reflected by the deceptive prism of our faulty
perceptions.

That our sight and mind play constant tricks is dramatized by an incident that seems unlikely yet psychologically
valid. The Narrator goes to Venice, fulfilling a boyhood
dream. It was the trip he had wanted to take when ill health
dictated the Norman sea coast instead. If Balbec then
marked the end of Gilberte and the beginning of Albertine,
Venice will now commemorate the end of Albertine.

But both Gilberte and Albertine are there!

He receives a communication that, hastily read, appears
to concern marriage and seems to be signed "Albertine." The
scrawled name is actually that of Gilberte, announcing her
engagement to Robert de St. Loup. Both comic and Kaf-
kaesque, this anecdote reveals the Narrator's uncertain
sensibility as he is at last "cured" of Albertine. Far from
Balbec, Paris, and Combray, on a distant, dreamed-of Adriatic shore, the passions of his life flare briefly and then die.
From the ashes emerge a new Gilberte, a new St. Loup, and
also a new Marcel.

In all of *Remembrance of Things Past,* there is no
richer demonstration of "successive selves" than the elusive
and contradictory Baron de Charlus. At first just a name in
the gossip of Combray, the Baron is mistakenly believed to
be Odette's lover. We later learn that he is actually a friend
of Swann's, who knows of his homosexuality and can there-
fore trust him to chaperone Odette. He appears as the Gentleman in White with her and Gilberte, and later as the
suspicious stranger at Balbec. Next comes the legend of the
Baron, half true, as told to the Narrator by Robert de St.
Loup. He portrays his uncle as a proud noble, steeped in

tradition, frequenting only the upper crust of the "upper crust," yet warmly disposed toward the lower classes—and also a notorious "lady killer." Actually, the Baron's warm impulses are directed primarily to young *men* of the working classes; his aloofness from society is based partly on snobbish exclusivity and partly on his preference for the "cities of the plain." The Narrator gradually recognizes the Baron's self-proclaimed virility as a pose. If the Baron genuinely detests effeminancy in men, it is because he likes his lovers virile. The Baron's given name, Palamède, is not only suitably archaic, it is inherently ironic; abbreviated to *Mémé,* it is the name French children call their grandmothers.

An accomplished dilettante, if not an intellectual, he is a connoisseur of Balzac, discoursing freely on the *Comédie Humaine* with blatant reference to one character called Vautrin, a covert homosexual. When attracted to young men of his own social caste, the Baron is likely to lure them with the promise of rare editions from his library. He has, in sum, two fatal obsessions: his noble origins and his inverted sexuality. As an awesome character in Proust's novel, these are his strength; as a man destined to suffering, they are his weakness. He is alternately silly and superb, mysterious and transparent. His outrageous behavior and his increasingly feminine mannerisms are obvious to those with eyes to see, but as Proust continually demonstrates, our perceptions of reality are severely limited. The Narrator himself does not fully grasp the complexities of the Baron's conduct until midway through the novel.

As *Cities of the Plain* opens, he has not yet become embroiled in his disastrous affair with Albertine. Outside his Parisian apartment, he observes an encounter between the Baron and the neighborhood tailor, Jupien. The Baron's curious actions at Balbec now become clear as he approaches Jupien, strikes up a conversation, and they eventually go indoors together. Although he catches a few words, the Narrator observes the scene essentially as mime, describing it in comic terms with an analogy to the bee approaching the flower. It is recorded as a botanist might note the sequence of a fertilization process, and indeed the two men do indulge in a contrived dumb show of attraction and seduction, more like members of a species than individuals.

This chance meeting will have far-reaching effects, although it is not to be the "great love" of the Baron's life. That love is a young violinist, Charles Morel, who is a protégé of Mme. Verdurin and who introduces the Baron into a social milieu that he would never, unless blinded by love, deign to frequent.

Here Proust's incomparable sense of parallel structure is expertly evident. The scene between the Baron and Jupien corresponds to the Narrator's observation, early in the novel, of Mlle. Vinteuil embracing her girl friend. In that first instance, Marcel was too young to understand; now, through an association of images (both are seen through a window), he perceives "Swann's Way" and the "Guermantes Way" in the shadow of Sodom and Gomorrah. Constructing still another parallel, Proust shows us a mighty Guermantes compromising his standards and sacrificing self-esteem exactly as Swann did when he pursued Odette into the world of the Verdurins. But where Swann made the accommodation, it is the Baron's sin of snobbish pride that causes his downfall.

He finds his rival, if not his match, in Mme. Verdurin, the epitome of reverse snobbery. With feigned disregard for aristocratic tradition, she sloughs off the Baron's title and chides him, as she had reproached Swann, for frequenting those "bores" of the Faubourg St. Germain. She errs further when she tries to imply that she is acquainted with the Duc de Guermantes; the Baron casually informs her that the Duc is his brother. Their repartée explodes into open warfare. Mme. Verdurin rather viciously asks him for the name of some "broken-down old noble" she might employ as a concierge; he advises against this, suggesting that her guests might prefer the company of the concierge to spending the evening with her.

It is the Baron who ultimately stages the great battle, and loses. Vying for Morel as *his* protégé, he offers to assemble the Parisian elite at Mme. Verdurin's to hear the violinist. But when the Baron's guests snub her, the hostess, she is understandably outraged. She not only denounces the Baron and his morals in their presence but strikes the severest blow by turning his lover Morel against him. This is a boldly dramatic scene in which everyone seems ignominious. Yet it is the tragicomic Baron who wins our sympathy, as he is silently escorted out by a faded figure with a glittering title, the Queen of Naples—a "broken-down noble" proudly extending a simple courtesy to one of her own.

So powerful are the scenes between the Baron and his bourgeois adversary (the Narrator calls them "skirmishes"), they tend to overshadow the Baron's other campaign, which has been the conquest of the violinist "Charlie" Morel. The pattern is a familiar one, following that of Swann in love and Marcel in love: the intensity of the lover's pursuit is proportionate to the unattainability of the loved one. An infatuated Baron de Charlus sees not the real Charles Morel, crass and opportunistic, but a divinity of his own creation. The Baron is morbidly jealous and possessive, but their affair does not approach the dramatic depths of Swann/Odette or Marcel/Albertine. Proust handles the Charlus/Morel interlude as a lighter variation on his theme, often with comic strains. When Morel, obviously seeking more time to himself, decides to go to night school and study algebra (!), the Baron insists he do his studying "at home"—in the Baron's own library. It is a vaudeville version of the prisoner motif.

The Baron de Charlus is perhaps Proust's most masterful creation and is widely regarded as one of the finest portraits in twentieth-century fiction. Toward the end of the novel, during a World War I sequence, we are given glimpses of the Baron and of Mme. Verdurin, both still selfishly blind to anything other than their own vain pursuits. Mme. Verdurin, reading the newspaper for social gossip, is annoyed by the sinking of the Lusitania; it spoils her breakfast. The Baron de Charlus stalks the boulevards, finding in the mayhem of wartime Paris an enchanted garden of attractive young soldiers for his pleasure. Both are incorrigibly consumed by their respective pleasures: society and sex, the Janus-headed monster of *Remembrance of Things Past*.

Relentlessly pursuing what might be called "the Verdurin way," an ambitious nobody will soon reach heights of social distinction of which even she had not dreamed. Fatalistically following "the Charlus way," the lofty Baron has persisted in a kind of moral suicide, ending in sadomasochism beyond the bounds even Proust had first envisioned in *Swann's Way*. Proust does not condemn the Baron's homosexuality in itself; he sees it as the weakness, the "tragic flaw" that blinds and enslaves a potentially superior being. Throughout the novel, we observe a startling yet inevitable metamorphosis. The eminent scion of an ancient race, defying gods and men, is transformed into a shattered shell. All that is constant is his weakness. His fate is that of another ancient "race," the descendants of Sodom.

While German bombs rain down, we find the Baron in a male brothel managed by Jupien, pursuing his particular pleasure: chained to a bed, being beaten, he begs to be persuaded that his "executioner" is a dangerous apache from the Paris underworld. Actually, he is a harmless young fellow hired by Jupien to play a role. It is the last illusion.

This mighty scene would border on melodrama were it not for Proust's firm command. In his hands, the greater truth of the Baron's inner character overshadows the somewhat contrived narrative situation. Some readers, however, balk at another development in the novel: the revelation that

Robert de St. Loup, theretofore heterosexual—or to all appearances so—is, like his uncle, homosexual. Proust, perhaps naively, perhaps rightly, believed in deterministic heredity, and attributed homosexuality to a Guermantes family strain. Proust was also a master ironist. One of his chief contentions is that we do not see the truth around us. Masked ourselves, we rarely penetrate the masks of others. What greater irony than the discovery that a close friend has been leading a secret life unknown to us. It is the perfect counterpart to the Narrator's vain efforts to learn the full truth about Albertine.

St. Loup's story runs sporadically through the novel from the second volume to the last. His early infatuation with an actress named Rachel follows the same pattern as Swann's and Marcel's affairs; possessive and jealous, he is consumed by passion for a creature of his own fabrication. He does not know—nor would he believe if it were proved to him—that Rachel began her career in a house of prostitution. Apparently not yet homosexual or else a master of deceit, he has chosen her as his mistress, and this is the only role in which he sees her. Much later, when Gilberte becomes Mme. de St. Loup, she attempts in her appearance and manners to resemble Robert's former mistress. The irony is that Robert is no longer interested in women at all.

The discovery of Robert's homosexuality is a cause of great chagrin to the Narrator. While not disapproving, he is nonetheless shaken to learn (in the course of his inquiries about Albertine) that the magnificent Robert de St. Loup, a Guermantes, could have made overtures to an elevator boy. It is final evidence that the gods of his youth are wholly human. Neither this nor the loss of Albertine, however, lie at the cause of that despair that Marcel feels as volume six and the Venice episode conclude. It is rather an all-pervading *Weltschmerz,* the sense that life has passed him by, that none of what has happened holds any meaning at all. He believed in turn that the Duchesse, Gilberte, and Albertine were permanent, unchanging entities, that his emotions would last forever. That we can love intensely, then no longer love, and finally no longer care—this is the ultimate disillusion, the work of devouring time he cannot face nor comprehend.

3

A Masked Ball

All that past I did not know
I bore within myself
—*M.P.*

Despite the powerful symmetry of its inner structure, *Remembrance of Things Past* is actually divided into two very uneven narrative sequences. The first six volumes record the events of the Narrator's relatively uneventful life through early manhood. The seventh and last volume, most of which takes place on a single day many years later, illuminates those events and that life in a dramatically unexpected manner. The French title of volume six, *La fugitive,* suggests not only the captive Albertine's flight but the flight of time itself, the passage of the Narrator's own life void of substance, shape, or meaning. All he seems to have known is the vacuum of loss. Volume seven, *Le temps retrouvé,* means both "the past recaptured" and "time recaptured." It is an affirmation of optimistic humanism.

In achieving his metaphysical intention, the triumph of human mind over time, Proust took great liberties with conventional chronology. During the first six volumes, we are essentially outside time. We are in a static yet fluid present which is the immediate consciousness of the Narrator. It is static in that our sole constant is his actual moment of recollection and reflection. Yet it is fluid insofar as his associative memories float freely from era to era of his life. The narrative does move forward and the Narrator does age, but chronological progress is subject to countless, often elusive, leaps backward and forward in time.

In the final volume, on the contrary, Proust observed a relatively recognizable calendar. *The Past Recaptured* is portioned into three segments with World War I as a frame of reference. At an indeterminate date, the mature Narrator visits Gilberte, and a path of reminiscence is explored. He then briefly states that during a long period he was in a sanitarium for his health. The length of his extensive absence from Paris can only be approximated. Yet during this period of confinement, the Narrator records two visits to the city (variously dated 1914 and 1916), noting the physical and social changes of an era. At a later, still indeterminate date, he spends a final day in the world of the Faubourg St. Germain. It is a day of apocalypse and revelation.

That single day, however, is not without preparation and prelude. One of the key scenes of the novel, though briefly drawn, is the opening passage of the final volume in which the Narrator describes his visit to his childhood sweetheart. Although it bears no clear temporal relationship to the events that precede or follow, it is absolutely germane to his ultimate understanding of his spiritual experience, the meaning of his existence, and the discovery of his vocation. The scene, for the first time since *Swann's Way,* is again Combray. In the very house to which he was forbidden access as a child, Swann's country manor Tansonville, the Narrator is the guest of Gilberte, now the Marquise de St. Loup and, by marriage, a Guermantes.

The worlds of his past have oddly and unexpectedly merged. It is not Proust's wont to overdramatize, however; the reader, more than the Narrator at this point, senses the impact of their fusion. While walking about the Combray countryside with Gilberte, he learns that the paths he once knew as Swann's Way and the Guermantes Way—epitomizing the two separate, inaccessible dream worlds of his youth—actually meet. In space now, just as in time, disparate universes are symbolically joined. This discovery, contrary to expectation, is not a source of joy. It seems rather a cold and disappointing fact, a pinprick to his earlier illusions. The river that flows there, which once seemed a mighty stream, now appears "shallow and ugly." His perspective is that of a middle-aged man looking at the past as an isolated entity, detached in time, separate and apart, stripped of mystery, irretrievably lost. The great lesson of time recaptured, the extratemporal fusion of past and present, is yet to be absorbed.

Two words dominate the long opening paragraph of

this last volume: *jadis* and *autrefois,* both of which mean essentially "in days gone by." The reader senses the great temporal and emotional distance between the Narrator's past and his present experience in recalling that past. We also share his confusion and chagrin, his sense of desperate bewilderment, as Gilberte now confesses that as a child she found him a very attractive lad and would willingly have been "accessible" to him, but when he seemed indifferent, she went off instead with Théodore, the grocer's boy. This conversation, in its cruelly quiet way, is the Narrator's first dramatic step back into the reality of the past.

Although it is not actually recapitulated, one of the book's first scenes is vividly suggested here; the reader smells the hawthorn of Combray and feels Marcel's budding sexuality. What he most desired could have been readily his, had he only known how to act and react. We are there again—at the novel's beginning—in Marcel's childhood. At a turning in the road, we see the Lady in White, Odette. But our vision of that scene is now colored by our present knowledge that she is also the Lady in Pink, his uncle's mistress as well as a cabaret girl in men's clothes in one of Elstir's paintings; she is not only Swann's "wicked" wife, but Gilberte's beautiful mother, and also Robert's mother-in-law, a totality of successive selves. As that faded photograph revives, we recognize, too, the Mysterious Gentleman with her. Reportedly Odette's lover at that time, the Baron de Charlus has since been seen as a blatant yet elusive homosexual, a warm friend and a vicious enemy, a prince and a fool, and ultimately as the willing victim of an erotic fraud, beaten with chains in a male brothel as Paris is bombed by moonlight. The future, though neither the Narrator nor we could know it then, was present in the past; the walls of time begin to crumble.

Finally there is Gilberte herself, an angelic child making an obscene gesture which at the time only baffled the young Narrator for whom it was intended. Nor did he understand that later on, those afternoons playing along the Champs-Elysées, his courtship was too vigorous, too jealously possessive. The innocent candor of his desire was his undoing; the adult Gilberte frankly tells him that his outright pursuit made her feel like a victim of the Inquisition. With this, he recalls Albertine once more and desolately measures the repeated cost of his blunders, how his loving urge to possess "prisoners" has only made of them "fugitives." It is the beginning of understanding.

His great chagrin is not so much that he has failed to capture Gilberte and Albertine but that he now no longer cares. The novelist writing a simple tale of love lost might well conclude here. The ending would be poignant, appropriately ironic and bittersweet. Proust, on the other hand, was writing a novel of *time* lost, and the Narrator's melancholy at this point is rooted in the awful recognition that time effaces everything, not only the love that brought us sorrow and disappointment but also the very emotions of love and sorrow. He feels eroded by the ravaging flow of time, an empty being, a life unfulfilled. The adult Marcel can make no more sense of life than could the child Marcel who was father to the man. Now middle-aged, he has never been able to materialize his early dream of becoming a writer. And this is perhaps the most bitter of his failures.

As he leaves Gilberte and retires to his room, he chooses a book to read. It is a volume of memoirs that records a milieu of Parisian society with which the Narrator himself is quite familiar, the salon of Mme. Verdurin. There is high praise in these pages for the exquisite taste and superb wit that reigned at the Verdurin soirées. Her dinner parties are meticulously described in brilliant realistic detail and represented as the ne plus ultra of social and artistic salon life. Marcel has always believed in the power of the recorded word, the authenticity of literature, yet here he finds his own recollections vastly at odds with those he is reading. He too has been a part of that fragment of social history, has observed its pettiness and vulgarity, the vanity of its scheming intrigues. He knows well the people, their secrets, their idiosyncrasies and shallowness. Following Gilberte's revelations, however, he distrusts his own capacities for understanding. He is convinced that it is he who is wrong, that the literary version of the Verdurins is the true and just one. Having miscalculated his relationships with Albertine and Gilberte, he now believes that he has also wrongly evaluated the Verdurins and their "clan"; he even goes so far as to regret that, lacking true powers of understanding and observation, he has once again missed out on something wondrous.

The Narrator's retreat to a sanitarium at this point in the novel seems in many ways a convenient narrative device to mark the passage of time. It might also be taken as a symbol of moral collapse and the possibility of regeneration. All the Narrator's forces have failed and want renewal. World War I was just such a period for European society as well, and there are those who regard *Remembrance of Things Past* primarily as a sociological chronicle. It would be dangerous to overstress such parallels, though; the simple truth is that Proust had never planned to include a wartime episode in the novel that he had been intently constructing since 1909. While these pages provide a record of colorful impressions and a striking portrait of the aging Baron, they are somewhat disruptive to the tight overall design of the novel ending in the great "masked ball" scene. This, we know for a certainty, he had clearly envisioned as the inevitable climax to his work.

On his return from the rest cure, finding the once familiar "Guermantes" on an invitation, the Narrator momentarily experiences the magic that name once conjured for him. But as he continues to stare at the name, it loses all incantatory power. He could not suspect that this idle excursion into his past, attending yet another reception given by the Princesse de Guermantes, would assume the near-apocalyptic proportions of a last judgment.

En route to the Guermantes reception, the Narrator has an encounter that seems to presage apotheosis, announcing in its way the novel's crowning theme of resurrection and redemption. Sitting on a park bench along the Champs-Elysées, there is the aged Baron de Charlus; although the scene is brief, it is mighty in its impact, comprehensive in its summation of Proustian ideas. His fertile imagination unable to resist the multiple metaphor, Proust successively compares the Baron to Oedipus, Neptune, King Lear, and a "big baby." Having suffered a stroke, the feeble Baron is now entirely in the care of Jupien; his sex partner and pander has become his nursemaid. Having almost lost both sight and mind, the Baron has now in large measure regained both, but his tottering body—he seems propped up rather than seated on the bench—is that of a fallen giant. His once proudly slick black hair has become a great white mane; his sweeping silvery beard suggests not only Lear but the statue of some sea god covered with snow. As a carriage passes, Jupien whispers to the Baron that its passenger is a lady of his former acquaintance, whereupon the Baron de Charlus slowly and unsteadily struggles, miraculously managing a deep and noble bow. The Narrator, observing the scene, marvels not only at this feat of physical prowess but the moral strength that animates it, and still further at the underlying irony, for the lady in the carriage is one whom the Baron had not only snubbed socially in years past but positively insulted. Whether he now recognizes her is not made clear; what counts is the measure of his response, the defiant capacity to summon his failing powers and coordinate them in a superb gesture that proclaims he is alive and in full command of himself.

It is a proud yet hollow gesture, a triumphant testimony
to the Baron's instinctive and unflinching nobility, but at the
same time a reminder of the fleeting vanity of human pride
and its offshoot, snobbery. If it is a mechanical gesture, how
great the human effort to implement that flagging mechanism. Since Proust, through the eyes of the wondering Marcel, focuses so intently on this scene, we must assume its
importance as embodying the complexity of human character. Throughout his many appearances, the Baron de Charlus has shown himself to be in turn generous and giving,
petty and malicious, brittly brilliant, caustic and sophisticated, and something of a pompous ass. We have seen him
in the role of authentic nobility and also reduced by his own
vicious folly to a pitiful state of bestiality. The Baron's salute
to Mme. Saint-Euverte is purposefully equivocal. Is he playing merely a part to the very last, or is there, after all, a
redemptive humility here? Though Proust does not invoke it,
there seems a structural parallel between this scene and that
earlier scene where the Baron was "rescued" in his shame at
the Verdurin salon by a proudly humble gesture on the part
of the Queen of Naples.

Which Baron de Charlus are we then to remember—the
haughty and vituperative "Mémé," the worldly aristocrat,
the hopeless pervert, chained and beaten, or the tottering
giant with the silvery mane? "M. de Charlus was indeed two
very different people," writes the Narrator with measured
understatement, "not counting his other identities." By way
of final contrast, still another juxtaposition is delineated.
Jupien confides to the Narrator that the Baron, left briefly
alone during the period of his blindness and convalescence
from paralysis, had mistaken the timbre of a male voice and
was discovered seducing a ten-year-old boy. "He's nothing
but a big baby himself," adds the Baron's guardian. Yet the
reader's last impression of this complex and contradictory
personage, faithful to his various selves, is that of a Lear-like

Baron, suddenly raising his voice from a barely audible stammer to intone, as though himself defying death, a majestic litany of friends and contemporaries no longer living: "Hannibal de Bréauté, dead! Antoine de Mouchy, dead! Charles Swann, dead! Boson de Talleyrand, dead! . . ."

This confrontation with the tangible ravages of time, however powerful its effect on the reader, does not yet seem to shake the Narrator. As he approaches the Guermantes mansion, however, he is beset by a curious succession of sensory experiences that prove ultimately more revealing than his encounter with the protean Baron. First, the Narrator's foot strikes against an irregular stone in the path, but in lieu of discomfort, he is inexplicably seized by an almost spiritual inundation of joy. Lost in a vision of azure and dazzling light, bathed in a strange, cool freshness, he is suddenly in Venice! That is to say, he experiences a total immersion, body, mind, and spirit, in the atmosphere of that Italian city which he briefly visited with such great pleasure but sought in vain to recapture through the conventional processes of memory. Now, two uneven steps leading to the Baptistery of St. Mark find their physical counterpart in the flagstones before the Guermantes mansion, and the Narrator is catapulted through space and time to another era and another place. It is not merely that the stones somehow *remind* him of Venice (this is no rudimentary experience of association and recollection); there is a total resurrection of past experience.

Just as the *madeleine* soaked in tea provoked a total resurrection of Combray ("towns, gardens, and everything"), this unwonted emergence of Venice is another demonstration of Proust's "involuntary memory." As though some mystic disposition had been triggered, the susceptible Narrator next experiences a comparable auditory sensation. Waiting in the Guermantes library to be announced and offered refreshment while he waits, he hears the sound of a spoon striking a plate, but its resonance for him is identical to that of a workman's hammer he had heard outside a train compartment. Present reality is again effaced, and he seems to be aboard that train, halted near a wood, observing a row of trees. A faint smell of smoke permeates the air, his own feeling of warmth is tempered by the cool green of the nearby forest. Oblivious to immediate surroundings and perceptions, he relives that experience.

Mechanically taking a napkin, he senses an all-pervading azure mass again sweep over him:

I felt as though the servant had just opened a window onto the beach, an invitation for me to stroll along the jetty at high tide; the napkin I had picked up to wipe my mouth had exactly that degree of stiffness and starchiness as the one I had such trouble with on my first day at Balbec. . . . Within its folds and creases, it spread before me, like a peacock's tail, the plumage of a blue-green sea.

The reincarnation this time is from a far more distant past. And it is at this moment of revelation that Proust's novel asserts clearly its metaphysical intention and assumes the decisive structure that has been implicit from the start, though evident perhaps to only the most perspicacious reader.

In seeking out the reasons why these extraordinary sensory perceptions should yield such emotions of joy, the Narrator concludes: "I was experiencing them simultaneously in both the present moment and in a distant moment, the past encroaching upon the present to the extent that I could not be sure in which of these I truly was. . . ." He seems to enjoy an authentic extratemporality, becomes another being outside time, immune to its ravages and even to those of death. Where the exercise of intelligence and conscious recollection fail, this experience of *involuntary* memory enables him to recapture bygone days, the past he had believed lost.

Thinking of the many times when immediate reality had been a source of disappointment, he realizes that the greatest pleasures lie in anticipation and in recollection. A daring metaphysic is posed here, counter to those trends of twentieth-century pragmatism that place such a premium on "now." Proust's system effectively denies the significant reality of present, extending forward in the realm of imagination, then backward, incorporating experience into the more permanent form of memory. More explicitly, Proust ventures to suppose a dimension in which past pervades present, creating a new and unprecedented domain of reality.

For Proust, this revivified presence is more "real" than when first experienced for it was then but a fleeting moment in time and now it has been recaptured in the form of time-defying permanence. We possess the past as part of us.

But is such a privileged experience, to know "a bit of time in its pure state," destined only to last for the flash of a moment? Our capacity to experience such moments "free from the rigors of time," Proust claims, implies an aspect of man that is also liberated from time. It is this line of reasoning that leads the Narrator to consider the importance of literature and the role of the creative artist.

Still waiting for the concert to end so that he may enter the salon, the Narrator casually leafs through a book. Its title is one, like the name Guermantes, that he has not thought about for years. But like that very name, it unleashes buried memories. It is a novel by George Sand, one that his grandmother had given him as a boy, about a foundling and his need for love. As he remembers his mother reading to him aloud, from its pages there suddenly stalks a stranger: "That stranger was myself, the child I was then. . . ." Another book, bearing a pompous, servile dedication to the Prince de Guermantes, is a novel by Bergotte, the writer he had worshiped and met at the Swanns. One winter's day when the weather had kept him from meeting Gilberte, he had contented himself with reading that very book. From its pages now fall the snows of yesteryear: "The snow that covered the Champs-Elysées that day has not vanished from the volume, I see it still."

For Marcel Proust, as the reader now vividly senses (along with an increasing identification between Marcel the Narrator and Proust the novelist), only a work of art can give to life shape, pattern, and meaning, only a book can redeem the formless, pointless past. It is significant that this scene of preliminary revelation takes place in a library setting. Yet it is also significant that the Narrator's ultimate enlightenment will occur in the world of the living.

The living he meets behind those doors, however, are the living dead. Assuming that his revelation of extratemporality is a kind of key to eternity, the Narrator is now faced once more with the shocking evidence of age, time, man's mortality. What he finds as he enters a Guermantes salon for the last time, in lieu of his once glittering magic-lantern dream, in lieu of the vapid cardboard world it proved to be, is a veritable wax museum: painted faces, bent bodies, a parade of ghosts at a macabre masquerade. The salon is like a hushed cemetery.

Just as the Opéra scene (the Narrator's first venture into society) was steeped in dreamlike aquatic metaphor, this scene (his farewell to the world of the Guermantes) suggests faded flora, decayed fauna. Proust consciously invoked a kind of surrealist imagery to convey its frightening irreality.

One man has grown to look so exactly like his father that the Narrator understandably confuses them. Another man falsely appears to have stayed young because his son, drastically aged, looks older than he. Snow-white beards like the Baron's are everywhere. When the charming young Duc de Châtellerault (once long ago announced by a footman who had had sex with him) now enters, the Narrator sees a little old man with the silvery mustache of an ambassador.

He recognizes a princess who had once indiscreetly made overtures to him. She still sports a coquettish air, but her face is cosmetically "embalmed" the color of lilac; still erect, not shriveled, she seems nonetheless a head shorter than when he first knew her.

Some guests, their faces unmarked by the years, are hardly able to walk or move. Age has rendered one gentleman totally unrecognizable except when he speaks; his voice seems a timeless phonograph record reproducing precisely the same sounds the Narrator remembers. In a stout gray-haired lady waltzing by, he identifies a pretty blonde from the past, but only because he is told her name. The name is all that remains of that memory. Another heavy-set woman approaches him directly, smiling. Is it Odette? "You're confusing me with my mother," says Gilberte. Odette herself seems miraculously unchanged, as though infused with a liquid wax that swells the skin without drastically altering the features. Like the princess with the lilac face, Odette seems a perennially preserved orchid.

Everyone seems to be wearing masks, though in many cases a mask of his own face. The Narrator sees them first not as elderly men and women but as young people grown incredibly faded. They seem parchment versions of their former selves, like dried fruits or flowers. In still another perspective, they appear as dolls, but nondimensional, more like the immaterial images projected by the magic lantern on the walls of his bedroom at Combray. It is time, he now understands, time made visible, which has stripped them of the material dimension, reduced them to this pale puppet dance. Which is the dance of death, for to live in time is to die. Only the transpositions of memory and imagination countermanding time, can restore these lives. It is a work of the mind, the viewer's mind. Only the subjective consciousness, in a simultaneous reconstruction of their past selves, a superimposition of his own mnemonic levels, can bring these

people back to life again and give them substance. It is thus
that the dead and the dying live—in us.

The Narrator's perception of his own identity suffers a
severe shock, as well. When Gilberte suggests they have
dinner, he thoughtlessly replies: "If you won't feel com-
promised dining alone in a restaurant with a young man."
Hearing laughter around them, he realizes that in the eyes of
others he has none of the youthful allure that he perceives in
the mirror of his mind. When someone later tells him, "You
haven't changed a bit," he understands this to mean, "How
you *have* changed!" Just as the Baron de Charlus, ever
dreaming of youthful virility, continually thinks of himself as
young and virile, the Narrator's own self-portrait is one of
youthful vigor. It is a false image. Intellectually, he is capable
of knowing we all age, but this is vain knowledge, for in our
efforts to arrest time and stave off death, we tend to see
people, including ourselves, in choice moments of past remembrance. It is an attempt to achieve permanence in the
ephemeral, fleeting world of time where the great *distances,*
for Proust, are not spatial but temporal.

The evidence of time's erosion, seen everywhere around
him, causes the Narrator to despair over his earlier hope that
he might create in fiction a reality outside the realm of time.
He must now take into account, as well, the work of time in
altering relationships as well as in distorting human flesh.
Following the curve of memory (here conscious or voluntary memory), he realizes that his childhood love, Gilberte,
is not only now a Guermantes through her marriage with his
friend Robert, she is in line to inherit the title, Duchesse de
Guermantes—his earliest childhood idol. He recalls that
Swann often dreamed of presenting his wife and daughter to
society through the Duchesse de Guermantes, but even
though she was his friend socially, the Duchesse would not
consent to such a breach of protocol. Now, through money,
Gilberte and the Duchesse are allied. Now, through the

breakdown of once prized values, the Duchesse entertains actresses including Rachel, Robert's former mistress and, prior to that, a whore.

The Duc himself, that ailing and antiquated "superb ruin," has been unfaithful to the Duchesse since the start of their marriage. If it seems incredible that at death's door he still maintains a mistress, it is more startling still to learn that the mistress who now keeps him company and cares for him is Odette. The relationship seems almost too much to accept, until we consider the nature of their respective psychologies: he has always had a mistress and she has always played the role of "kept woman." Age does not modify but only serves to ingrain the forces of habit. There is a certain inevitability in this ludicrously touching twilight affair. Like the Baron de Charlus, they are mechanically faithful to their folly and their vice, faithful to an inner core self that remains constant amidst the cascade of successive selves.

To some readers, the spectacular moment of Proust's last volume is the revelation—in true masked-ball style—that the Princesse de Guermantes is not *the* Princesse de Guermantes, paragon of Parisian society, but Mme. Verdurin, who has completed her climb to the top. Her jovial, pipe-smoking husband is dead, and the wealthy widow Verdurin at last acquires her "ruined noble" by virtually "buying" the Duc de Duras, a minor Guermantes, as her second husband. On his death, she is in an excellent position to save the widowed and financially ruined Prince de Guermantes by marrying him. She thus becomes a cousin to the Duchesse—and her superior in social rank!

There is indeed a consummate irony here, especially when the Narrator discovers that most people think of the new Princesse only as a former Duchesse, blind to her origins as the "bourgeois-bohemian" Mme. Verdurin. In another instance of history revised, Odette is thought of as the widow of M. de Forcheville. Swann's memory—except in the Narrator's own memory—is fading into oblivion. Although they were once fast friends, the Duchesse de Guermantes virtually denies ever having known Swann, just as she had once denied him the courtesy of her receiving Odette and Gilberte. Gilberte, in order to suppress her Jewish ancestry, has also made a conscious effort to disassociate herself from Swann's name and his life. She is now a Guermantes. Yet when she tells the Narrator how boring she finds the stuffy salon life and invites him to her own informal artistic circle, she sounds exactly like the Mme. Verdurin of yesteryear!

These social and psychological ramifications clearly do fascinate Proust, but they provide only the framework and not the inner theme of his work. There will always be a Princesse de Guermantes; someone or other, worthy or not, will hold that title, as well as the once enchanting title, Duchesse de Guermantes. This is an historical progression, a role maintained and played by a succession of different persons. Proust is less concerned with social and historical progression than with life cycles, movement backward and forward in time. The true revelation of the Guermantes reception, and of *The Past Recaptured,* is not the costumed skeletons or the bourgeois wearing the masks of nobles; it is the resurrection of his own lost youth and the redemption of his lost, fragmented past in the guise of a child aged sixteen, the daughter of Gilberte and Robert de St. Loup.

Slowly, though not always clearly, as we have seen, the pieces of an incomprehensible puzzle, the Narrator's life, seem to be beginning to fit. Then, periodically, the vision loses coherence. When Gilberte now brings her daughter to meet Marcel, it is clear in a flash of illumination that it is this young girl who provides the key to his life's meaning. The people present at the reception afford the Narrator's memory ample play for an examination and reevaluation of his past, but it is Mlle. de St. Loup who truly incorporates all the many varied "transversals," as he calls them, for the total recapitulation of his life pattern. Her mother represents Swann's Way, her father the Guermantes Way. It is not only in space that the two paths of Marcel's childhood are seen to meet (and prove a disappointment to him) but also in time, which is a source of revelation and joy.

If it was at Balbec that Marcel first met the girl's father, Robert de St. Loup, it was her grandfather Swann who had urged him to go there. It was through Robert, and so indirectly through Swann, that he first met the Duchesse with whom he had fallen in love at Combray. Balbec had also introduced him to the Baron, ever a symbol of mystery and identified with the mysteries of Albertine. The Baron had loved Charlie Morel, a musician of some genius, but also a plotter and a schemer, who had later been the lover of the Baron's nephew—the father of Mlle. de St. Loup. The child's grandmother, Odette, was of course Mme. Swann, but she was also the mistress of Marcel's uncle. And it was Morel, the son of his uncle's valet, who became a kind of "mistress" to both the Baron and Robert.

Condensed to a paragraph, the incidence of coincidence seems staggering, untenable. We must bear in mind that this accumulation of associations is spun out in the shape of fiction over seven volumes totaling thousands of pages, and that it represents in fictional *time* half a lifetime of experience. *The Past Recaptured* is the pivotal volume on which the entire work turns, and it does turn, as we might expect, back to the past for a fresh beginning. No words are spoken between the Narrator and Mlle. de St. Loup. None are needed; there are none. She is, quite simply, the necessary symbol of his own life: "I found her altogether lovely: still full of hope and laughter, made up of the years that I had lost, she recaptured my youth."

She is the key to his life and the key to his book that, just a few pages later, comes to an end—and yet begins again. As the Narrator decides to recapture his life in its telling, we are once again back at Combray where a lonely boy projects magic-lantern images against the wall of his room. Although the middle-aged Narrator is in the Guermantes salon, face to face with Swann's granddaughter, he seems to hear the bell on the garden gate. The bell rings and Swann arrives in memory, talks of art and of far-off places. The present becomes the past and the past present; time is defeated and transcended. A boy sits on a hill reading a book and cannot hear the church bells because he is lost in the world of the book. He smells the deliriously sensual odor of hawthorns, sees a pretty blonde girl named Gilberte with a Lady in White and a mysterious Gentleman in White. And they are all, including now Mlle. de St. Loup, the people of the book he will write, which is the book of his life.

He does not yet know the mystery and the suffering that Albertine will bring, and by the time his book ends he will be free of her. But all of the people, all of the suffering and the mystery he has known, will be projected through the magic lantern of the novel he will write. The little boy in the room has matured into a man, a man in a room writing a book about the little boy.

4

The Light
in the Window

Forever gone?
—*M.P.*

There are three fictional artists who play prominent roles in *Remembrance of Things Past:* a writer, a painter, and a musician. While none is really a leading character, like the Baron de Charlus or Gilberte, the lives and works of each are closely related to the events of Marcel's life and to his own emergence as a creative artist. So tightly knit is Proust's design that the composer Vinteuil, the painter Elstir, and the novelist Bergotte, represent not only three spheres of aesthetic experience but also correspond to the worlds in which the Narrator moves and to stages of his emotional evolution.

Vinteuil's name is part of the Combray town gossip because of his lesbian daughter. Her defiant behavior is said to have caused the old music teacher much suffering, perhaps contributed to his death. It is at Mme. Verdurin's that Vinteuil's sonata is introduced, winning him a posthumous hearing. Her selfish ambition for social distinction, a chic "artistic" salon, results in eventual fame for an obscure artist. At the same time, his music provides a backdrop for Swann's pursuit of Odette; the "little phrase" of the Vinteuil sonata symbolizes Swann's love.

In the great scene where the Baron and Mme. Verdurin clash, the evening's musical event is the premiere of a newly discovered Vinteuil septet. This time it is the Narrator who is affected. He observes Mme. Verdurin in her studied pose of pained ecstasy, he senses the indifference of most guests to the music, the tense animosity between the two social castes. Watching Morel the violinist and his genuinely ecstatic lover, the Baron, he reflects on the futility of his own affair with Albertine, the overall vanity and chaotic hopelessness of human existence. Only the music seems to provide pattern and meaning.

Thus, starting in *Swann's Way* and continuing over a series of volumes, seemingly unrelated references to Vinteuil and his daughter are now seen as integral to Proust's themes of love and art. Mlle. Vinteuil offers a first glimpse into the world of Sodom and Gomorrah; the composer provides an initiation into the realm of art where the Narrator will find his ultimate revelation, his solace and fulfillment.

In this key scene, where characters from the Narrator's various worlds are represented, we find a subtly wrought intersection of plot lines and themes, reflected in the complex counterpoint of the music. Several levels of the novel's meaning—social, artistic, psychological and philosophical—meet and form a design. As the "little phrase" of Vinteuil's sonata suddenly emerges newly orchestrated in the richer, more colorful harmonies of the Vinteuil septet, we realize too that Proust is dramatizing his own aesthetic of the novel.

The writer Bergotte is identified primarily with Paris and the world of Gilberte. The Narrator, a boy with a taste for literature, has discovered a new idol and is hurt when a family friend dismisses Bergotte as a "flute player," a facile stylist with no substance. It is one of the first instances in which the Narrator is made to reflect on aesthetic problems, the relationship between meaning and form. He feels, but does not yet understand; he is simply captivated by the subtle cadences of Bergotte's nuanced manner.

The fact that Gilberte Swann, his other idol, actually knows Bergotte seems a joy impossible to bear. When she gives him a copy of Bergotte's book on theater, it becomes a doubly treasured possession. But when he meets Bergotte, at luncheon with the Swanns, it is a gross disappointment. Marcel's image of a venerable white-haired sage explodes on confrontation with the real Bergotte, a youngish red-faced man with a bulbous snail's shell nose, who makes fatuous conversation and biting remarks about other guests after the party. Gods do not look or behave like that. Marcel prefers books and illusions.

While Bergotte plays no great role in the progress of Proust's novel, we hear from time to time of his life and

career. The wily Mme. Verdurin tries to make him the
"catch" of her salon, but it is Odette Swann who succeeds
in creating a literary circle around Bergotte, using him to
further her own social ambitions. Proust also uses Bergotte
to depict the dichotomy of the artist whose personal life is
totally divorced from his artistic achievement. That the high
moral tone of Bergotte's work is not reflected in his private
morality surprises one of the characters in *Remembrance of
Things Past*. Proust quite clearly sees no legitimate connec-
tion.

He attributes to Bergotte this defensive paradox: "I
spend more than a multimillionaire on my little mistresses
but from the delights and deceptions they afford me, I have
the material for books which in turn bring me money." His
health and creative forces failing, Bergotte retires from the
social whirl into silence; his death scene is simply but im-
pressively recounted. Managing to leave his bed to attend an
exhibition, his eye focuses on a favorite painting by Vermeer, and in particular on a patch of exquisitely rendered
yellow in which layers of hues create a vivid impression of
depth: "That's how I should have written. My last books
were too dry, they needed thicker coats of color." Bergotte
dies muttering "little patch of yellow," which is symbolic,
like the deep coloring of Vermeer's painting and Vinteuil's
music, of art's potential richness and complexity.

As a character in his own right, Elstir appears as a
"succession of selves." First lionized by the Verdurins, he is
known more for his personality than his talent. Later, when
his paintings hang in museums and are collected by the
Guermantes, Mme. Verdurin alternately claims to have discovered him and to find his work insignificant. He enters the
Narrator's life when the boy, vacationing at Balbec, uses
Swann's name to gain admission to the now celebrated
painter's studio. While there, he stumbles on a startling discovery: a portrait of Odette in men's evening clothes. Was

she Elstir's model, his mistress? Did she, as Swann had heard, frequent lesbians? These are the taunting mysteries of others' lives, lives and mysteries we are destined never fully to fathom. It is also through Elstir that the young Narrator meets Albertine; yet the most durable outcome of the boy's encounter with Elstir is his dawning grasp on an aesthetic code, his understanding of a new way of seeing.

Elstir believes in, and succeeds in capturing on canvas, the immediacy of his perceptions, free from intrusive intellectual reflection. That is, he reproduces form and tonality of color exactly as his eye records them at a given moment. It does not matter if that vision is wholly subjective, elusive, and transitory, the artist illuminates reality, giving it permanence, and in so doing, enables others to see the world in new ways. Elstir's knowledge that the sea is fluid, his habitual vision of the sea as blue, are not allowed to interfere if in a circumstance of lighting at his particular moment of perception, it appears as a solid orange mass.

In observing Elstir at work and talking with him, the young Narrator learns that conditioned preconceptions may actually hinder our vision, that what we think of as mere optical illusions may be as valid to our experience as what we traditionally call reality. Stripped of the prejudice of intellectualizing, the artist may go directly to the heart of an alternate, more viable, reality. The essence of Elstir's philosophy will not truly be recaptured until later in the Narrator's life, and Elstir forewarns him: "Wisdom is not handed down to us, each of us must discover it for himself during the course of a journey that no one else can take for us and no one can spare us, for wisdom is a point of view, a way of seeing things." Eventually, the rich complexity of Vinteuil's music, the subtle levels of Bergotte's prose, the transcendent reality of Elstir's vision all contribute to the shaping of the Narrator's own aesthetic; they are the qualities he will seek to capture in recapturing his own past in art.

But at the moment of Elstir's lesson, he is only half-listening; he is watching Albertine and the girls of Balbec. Sensuality is real and immediate; aesthetic theory seems distant and abstract.

Did Proust have particular models in view when he created these three artists? Critical speculation is rife, and idle. The fictional names Vinteuil and Elstir suggest no historical counterparts. Bergotte strongly suggests Henri Bergson whose books on philosophy popularized the theory that the perception of reality is a subjective phenomenon—an idea to which Proust was altogether sympathetic. Bergson, however, wrote no fiction, and in Proust's novel, it is Bergotte's style rather than his thought that attracts the Narrator. Most critics conclude that Bergotte is patterned on Anatole France, whom Proust knew and esteemed.

Concerning Vinteuil's musical style, we have the confirmation of Proust's correspondence that the "little phrase" was inspired by various composers of his era: Fauré, Franck, Saint-Saens, even Wagner. Rather than the mode of one artist, Vinteuil's seems a distillation of period styles. In like manner, Elstir's "modern" aesthetic suggests that of the cubist and impressionist schools. It was, at the turn of the century, a new mode of vision, subjective rather than photographic or representational.

Essentially, each of the artists in *Remembrance of Things Past* is a fictional creation, parts of a synthesis representing Proust's own attitudes on aesthetics and the creative vocation. Vinteuil, like countless artists, attains fame only posthumously. He is also portrayed, a trifle sentimentally, as a prototype of the artist whose personal suffering brings greater depths to his work. Bergotte's life serves as a warning to the artist who permits himself to be lionized by society. It is implied that his creative forces are squandered, that the quality of his work diminishes. Conversely, Elstir demonstrates the wisdom of withdrawing from the world in total dedication to one's art. It is unlikely that he would have been so productive as a continued habitué of the Verdurin clan; his retirement to a studio on the sea coast was requisite.

No architect is portrayed in the novel, but Proust, in conversation and correspondence, frequently referred to the "architecture" of *Remembrance of Things Past*. After the first few volumes had appeared, he was angered that some critics found it shapeless and digressive. Since the total structure, except to informed or highly intuitive readers, is not altogether apparent prior to the "revelation" scene in *The Past Recaptured*, we may perhaps forgive early readers' ignorance of the novel's inherent design. Proust even considered naming various sections after the structural units of a cathedral such as portico, nave, apse. Such a pretentious artifice seems uncalled for, although the analogy itself is sound.

A cathedral is a monumental construction celebrating joy and sorrow, life, love and death, sin, redemption and resurrection. It is by nature panoramic, recording lives and legends and consecrating their memory through the relative permanence of art. Although its chapels, dome or spire, its sculpted doors and stained-glass windows, may be regarded as separate entities and admired for their detailed workmanship, the composite structure assumes a massive and coherent totality. And a cathedral is symbolic of a vision. It was in just such terms that Proust conceived his novel. An early clue is provided in the episode where the young Narrator expresses his disappointment on seeing the church at Balbec. But when Elstir describes it as an artist, recreating it for him in terms of form and aesthetic values, he perceives its essential "reality."

It is wrong, as some critics do, to limit our conception of Proust to that of a high priest of art who made a cult or religion of the creative act. While he did perceive art as a

transcendent reality, and the ritual of writing as near sacra-
mental, Proust's novel is also rooted in humanity, very vital
humanity, at virtually every level of human concern and
experience. Perhaps more than a "cathedral," *Remembrance
of Things Past* may be compared to that other medieval
form, the *summa,* an all-inclusive compendium incorporating the observations and the knowledge of a point in historical time. Recorded as a diary of the memory, the novel
embraces both the spiritual autobiography of one man and
the spirit of the age in which he flourished. Yet despite
historical specifics and the extreme sensibility of the Narrator, the reader easily relates to the patterns of desire and
illusion, frustration and despair, that compose the fictional
Marcel's life. These are universal quantities.

Proust's work may be read as a personal testament, as
history or sociology, as a study in psychology or philosophy,
as a moral treatise. His central stance remains that of the
artist, a novelist portraying people. But it is also that of a
man who faced a prospect known to all men, the idea that
we may die without having understood the value and the
meaning of our lives. In a long soliloquy on life and art,
Proust attributes these thoughts to the Narrator: "My whole
life had been like that of a painter, climbing a long path that
looks out on a lake, but the view is hidden by a blanket of
rocks and trees. Through a gap he can perceive it, he has it
all there before him and takes up his brush. But already
night is falling, the darkness too great to paint, that night on
which no day will ever rise."

The frame of reference is necessarily aesthetic, for the
premise of the entire novel is that of Marcel's discovery that
his own life has been the evolution of the artistic vocation.
Yet Proust, in a cannily contradictory aside, took great care
to include all mankind, not merely the elect artist in his
revelation of redemption: "Real life, life ultimately revealed
and illuminated, hence the only life truly experienced, is

literature; that life which, in a sense, is not only the artist's but with which every man is endowed." Like the artist, prior to his "illumination," we are hindered in a hundred ways—by habit, conditioning, prejudice, and like distortions of perception—from ever comprehending the true pattern and quality of our individual existence. Dulled, we do not even seek to see.

What style becomes for the writer, or color and form for the painter, is all a question of "vision," and this is accessible to every man, the possibility of seeing his own poor life not as desperate and void of direction, but the coherent accomplishment of an individual destiny, the recognition and the embrace of our personal mythology. Each of us is a book, and potentially, perhaps, a legend.

Few of us will compose poems or novels, still-lifes or sonatas, yet Proust seems to urge us, like Freud in his revolutionary technique of psychoanalysis or Wordsworth in his *Ode: Intimations of Immortality from Recollections of Early Childhood*, to penetrate and seize our past in order to make more meaningful our present, to conceive the pattern and order of our life. When he describes the function of "true art," Proust simultaneously sums up his own scrupulously constructed aesthetic vision and a more universal philosophic code: " . . . to rediscover and recapture, to bring to the threshold of comprehension that reality which is so distant from the daily lives we lead, from which we progressively separate ourselves by erecting impenetrable barriers of conventional cognition, that reality which we may very well die without ever understanding, which is, quite simply, our own life."

For the most part fatalistic, often pessimistic to the point of cynicism, Proust nonetheless entertains a resolute belief in man, man as an individual perhaps more than the species man. When the Narrator's forward-looking quest takes a circular sweep back to the past, it is incumbent upon him to make sense of what has happened during his lifetime. A pattern is there and he must discover it; this is his only salvation. If the coherence he bestows upon the people, places, and events of his experience should be yet another illusion, let it be the greatest illusion of all. He must metamorphose that illusion into the form of a superior reality, his own legend. The alternative is chaos.

The process is purely subjective; it is what he himself has perceived of the world: *his* life, *his* legend, *his* myth. In the realm of moral issues, Proust neither chastens nor condemns, he merely demonstrates. He poses a dilemma shared with other artists from Sophocles to O'Neill: how much truth can we bear? If illusion is a prison, how much freer are we, how much happier, when stripped of our illusions? Acceptance of our life as ours is the ultimate act of identity and our sole salvation. If love is a fantasy, communion with others an unattainable longing and a delusion, if time surely erodes our lives and death is birth's twin, we have nothing to rely on but self, our mortal self. This being so, Proust's seeming pessimism is the ultimate humanism, a celebration of individual man.

God is absent from Proust's metaphysics. The concept of deity is simply not a factor in the Proustian life equation. There is, however, a body of critical thought that would endow Proust's work with religious significance. Generally, the argument runs that an artist so steeped in the cognizance of sin, the vanity of human values, futility and despair, must necessarily be seeking God. The same rationale is sometimes used to interpret the superbly decadent poetry of Baudelaire. It simply will not wash here. While there is a certain nostalgia for lost innocence and virtue, there is no indication in *Remembrance of Things Past,* nor yet in Marcel Proust's personal records, of the need for God. It is true, however, that two facets of his heredity, part Jewish and part Catholic, do seem to assert themselves: through a certain Old Testament tonality with respect to judgment and retribution, a New Testament charity for the wrongdoer and the possibility of redemption.

A prime example of Christian grace would be the Baron de Charlus. His final salute to Mme. de Saint-Euverte is intended by Proust to demonstrate the vanity of social snobbishness, but it also stands implicitly as a gesture of personal expiation. The Baron is neither penitent nor contrite in any literal religious sense; nor does it matter to what degree he may even be fully conscious of his act. Whatever the motivation, his monumental pride has acceded to a kind of humility. He is both testifying to his own nobility and redeeming himself for the barbarous insults he had once lavished on Mme. de Saint-Euverte. When he humiliated her (a scene that takes place in *Cities of the Plain*), she offered a provisional forgiveness, declaring: "No sin is without mercy." When, in the final volume, he salutes her "as though she were the Queen of France," atonement is complete. Further light is shed on the episode if we recall that it was the Queen of Naples who majestically helped the Baron save face in his own humiliation by Mme. Verdurin.

Although Proust frequently ridicules man's follies with biting wit, his sense of morality is warmly human—and simple in that it embraces the fundamental complexity of human nature. As in Christian theology, man's soul is a battleground between good and evil. The Verdurins, for all their selfish and uncharitable behavior, see fit to provide a pension for one of their "clan," whom they had often made a public whipping boy. They do this secretly, seeking no recognition, but they do so in the knowledge that the man is not destined to live long. The unqualified purity of the saint is not to be found in Proust's novel.

One of the simplest yet most complex Proustian characters is Françoise, the housekeeper at Combray who joins the Narrator's family after his Aunt Léonie dies. Never center stage, she is nonetheless a constant presence throughout, a curious combination of Sancho Panza and a Greek chorus. A hard-core realist, she does her best to debunk Marcel's quixotic illusions. Yet she herself is emotionally subject to illusions of another sort, seeing life only through the peephole of her prejudices, her very pronounced likes and dislikes. She finds the Baron gentle and generous, a very "good influence" on young Morel who does not fully appreciate his benefactor. She is blind to the homosexual relationship, but intuitively right in her appraisal of the violinist's opportunistic exploitation of the Baron.

Françoise is also inherently hypocritical. Although she goes through the outward motions of sympathy for a pregnant servant girl, she is privately vicious toward her. She has no use for Albertine, whom she instinctively senses to be "bad" for the Narrator, yet for Albertine's death she sheds tears accompanied by platitudes. She is, in short, human. Since she has been for so long a part of his daily life, Marcel imagines Françoise helping him with the more routine tasks an artist faces in writing a book. Although she is by then old and going blind, she would be the one to make sure his notes and the pages of his manuscript are kept in some kind of order. He recalls, too, that Françoise has been an artist in her own right, preparing culinary masterpieces with meticulous care and the true artist's intuition for ingredients in their just proportion. He wonders if he cannot learn from her as well as from Vinteuil, Bergotte and Elstir.

The Narrator has always paid close attention to the colorful and archaic flavor of her speech, for it seems to reflect, despite errors of grammar and syntax, a natural gusto and richness absent from contemporary French. Commenting on love, the uninhibited Françoise quotes a verse from her native province:

Who falls in love with a dog's behind,
The smell of roses there will find.*

In all of Proust's penetrating pages of analysis, there is perhaps no more succinctly poetic rendering of a basic truth. The delusions suffered by Swann, Charlus, and Marcel are laid bare in that coarse fragment of peasant wisdom.

The very name Françoise embodies France, steeped in centuries of wisdom and tradition. On numerous occasions, the Narrator likens the brash coarseness of the Duc and Duchesse that lies beneath their glossy veneer to the peasant hardiness of Françoise. He reminds us that the Guermantes, far back in time, were feudal lords and thereby closer to the soil than to the Faubourg St. Germain. Indeed the last portrait in the novel, the face the Narrator last remembers even after Mlle. de St. Loup, is that of the Duc de Guermantes. This seems an extraordinary stroke considering the relatively secondary role the Duc has played throughout. He ironically contrasts that "superb ruin" with his brother the Baron, reduced to lowering himself before a woman of inferior station. Now the Narrator watches the Duc himself rising on faltering legs, like an aged archbishop weighed down by a metal cross, but also as though towering on stilts, precariously perched above earth with no visible means of support but his defiant inner strength. The Duc, suddenly in the spotlight, becomes a kind of Everyman, noble and vulgar, callous and kind, Proust's symbol of contradictory humanity, and of man's unflinching vitality in the face of death.

Since Proust wrote *Remembrance of Things Past* primarily to convey a vision, it is not surprising that he uses a great many figures of optical instruments, ways of seeing. Critic Roger Shattuck has devoted a book-length study to his

* Qui du cul d'un chien s'amourose,
  Il lui paraît une rose.

interpretation of Proust's abundant optical imagery. There is, first off, the magic lantern that turns the Narrator's boyhood bedroom into a theater of the imagination. His figurative "dreams" are literally projected onto the walls of the room where he sleeps. In the first few pages of *Swann's Way,* there are also metaphorical references to the kinetoscope, which isolates moments of movement into separate photographic frames, and to the kaleidoscope, which produces varicolored symmetrical forms in ever-changing patterns. The kinetoscope may be likened to Proust's manner of arresting motion to examine and reflect, the kaleidoscope to the incessant and mystifying modulation of "successive selves." Different as they are, both instruments are artificial man-made devices to capture modes of reality. Such references are altogether prevalent, culminating in the microscope-telescope allusion that appears in the concluding pages.

Despite his protestations, Proust does seem at times to be applying a microscopic analysis, not only recording in detail his characters' words or gestures and their effect on the Narrator, but also the minutiae of psychological mutations, noting, for example, every nuance and gradation in Marcel's vacillating "love" for Albertine. It is true, however, that the telescope image ultimately prevails. The last words of *The Past Recaptured,* following immediately on the portrait of the Duc, sum up Proust's far-reaching aesthetic aim: to depict men not in spatial but temporal terms as "giants stretched out over the years, simultaneously touching widely distant epochs," occupying a vast and transcendent place in time.

Among all the elaborate visual metaphors contrived by Proust to communicate his concept of "vision," one of the most obvious and most frequent figures in the novel is, quite simply, the window. At Combray, there is the window from which the bed-ridden Aunt Léonie commands her narrow view of the universe, the window of the bathroom in which the young Narrator reads and masturbates, looking out on an old tower and on the field where Gilberte sometimes strolls. There is also the window through which he observes Mlle. Vinteuil and her friend. The window of the hotel dining room (surrealistically conjured in that over-starched napkin) takes in the sweep of the sea and the panorama of life at Balbec.

It is from a window that the Narrator spies on the Baron de Charlus and Jupien, discovering a hidden aspect of the Baron's secret life. The window on which Swann mistakenly raps, searching for Odette, has its counterpart in the window of Albertine's room at the Narrator's apartment. Returning home one night, he observes from the street an odd play of light creating the illusion of prison bars there. Within that visual metaphor, he realizes clearly for the first time that it is he, not Albertine, who is the captive prisoner.

For the most part, the Proustian window figure thus appears related to sexual imagery. One window, however, in a powerfully memorable moment of *Remembrance of Things Past,* symbolizes sublimation and transcendence. When Bergotte dies, Marcel as a frustrated writer himself raises the question of art and immortality: *Mort à jamais?* Dead for all time? It is the very same question he had raised early in the novel when he sets out in pursuit of his Combray childhood memories. The question is rhetorically posed, never probed nor specifically answered, for in turn the great religious question would be raised. But on the night of Bergotte's burial, the Narrator records: " . . . all through the night of his funeral, his books, arranged by threes in lighted windows, watched over like angels with spread wings, seeming for him who was gone the symbol of his resurrection."

In the final pages of *The Past Recaptured,* the Narrator

again poses the question of art's eternity, its power to immortalize. Despite a skeptical footnote at the bottom of that page, one may conjecture that Proust himself believed in the light in the window.

5

The Dandy
and the Monk

A work of art was the only means
of recapturing time gone.
—*M.P.*

There is a photograph of Marcel Proust in 1891 strumming a tennis racquet as though it were a banjo. One would hardly identify this twenty-year-old dandy, hair slicked down and wearing a dapper little mustache, with either the fictional Narrator of *Remembrance of Things Past* or the Marcel Proust of forty, who had virtually withdrawn from society and was feverishly struggling against failing health to complete his novel. The fear that death would come before he finished is the very emotion experienced by the Narrator at the Guermantes matinée as he ruminates the book he plans to write. So many are the parallels between author and Narrator, it was once commonly believed that the novel was autobiography, at best thinly veiled. Proust insisted otherwise, and after faithfully interpreting his express philosophical and aesthetic intentions, we must inevitably concur. The novel is not so much a recording of actual experiences as the transcribed record of an inner experience.

During the course of Proust's novel, the Narrator's family name is never mentioned. Only twice is "Marcel" used, both times by Albertine. In the first instance we find this parenthetical observation: ". . . she would say 'My' or 'My darling' followed by my baptismal name, which, attributing to the narrator the same first name as the author of this book, would have been 'My Marcel' or 'My darling Marcel.'" Proust was clearly determined to maintain a dichotomy between himself and the "hero" of *Remembrance of Things Past*.

Proust himself was homosexual; the Narrator is not. Proust was half Jewish; the Narrator is not. A few critics still contend (and the uninformed reader might assume) that Proust, in using the narrative "I," was simply hiding his identity in a deceitful effort to portray an idealized self. While this superficial conjecture contains an element of truth, the matter is more complex. In order fully to understand Proust the man and Proust the artist, we must trace the evolution of both, considering the relationship of each to that third persona, the fictional Narrator of *Remembrance of Things Past*. We should bear in mind that the era in which the novel was conceived and written had a far different social climate than our own. But even more importantly, Proust resolutely believed that the artist, when he is in the process of creating, becomes a different self from the one who eats, drinks, makes love, and moves about in the everyday world.

Marcel Proust was born on 10 July 1871, not in the heart of Paris where he spent the greater part of his fifty-one years, but in suburban Auteuil. His parents had fled there the previous winter, to the villa of Mme. Proust's uncle, when the events of the Franco-Prussian War had made the city itself unsafe. Although they soon returned to Paris, Proust's fictionalized recollections of family life stem from both his childhood visits to Auteuil and to the home of his paternal relatives in provincial Illiers. A child of delicate health, he was fiercely attached to his mother. And while Combray reflects the physical décor and atmosphere of Illiers, the emotional experiences of the Combray episode are largely based on his memories of the maternal relatives of Auteuil. This may be seen as a typically Proustian instance of autobiographical matter distilled and recreated in terms of fiction.

He also exercised the option of making his Narrator an only child, while in point of fact Marcel Proust had a younger brother who was destined, like his father, to become a successful and celebrated physician. Their combined medical knowledge, however, could not save Marcel from the lifetime tortures of asthma. At the age of nine, returning to Auteuil from the nearby Boulogne Wood (where the elegant society figures of his novel stroll and take carriage rides), he suffered his first siege of suffocation. This affliction, coupled with an extreme hypersensitivity, made of him a semi-invalid, not merely during the last years of his life, but throughout most of his years.

In our post-Freudian enlightenment, even the layman is quick to relate Proust's physical condition to his maternal dependence, and this, in turn, to his homosexuality. Whatever validity such oversimplification might have, Proust was too consciously an artist for us to reduce his work to case-book status. While he may have "suppressed" his brother, together with his sexual inversion and his mother's racial ancestry, for personal reasons, he did so too for creative reasons.

In creating fiction, Proust borrowed abundantly from his first-hand knowledge of homosexuality and his status as half-Jew. By making of his hero an Aryan heterosexual, however, he achieved a far greater measure of universality. For Proust, as we have seen, sought to write neither a social tract nor a plea for tolerance, but essentially a philosophical novel embracing what Montaigne and Pascal before him, and André Malraux after him, have called "the human condition."

It is something of a convention in autobiography or fictionalized biography to record one's school days. This is an aspect of the Narrator's life that is left untouched. It is not a part of his spiritual record; it presumably might have diverted the reader's attention from the Combray and Gilberte episodes.

The school Marcel Proust attended was not only one of the more elite Parisian lycées but was at that time the most "literary." There he was encouraged in his desire to write, although he was frequently criticized for run-on sentences! The model of French style is clarity and concision; yet Proust, even as a boy, was already tentatively shaping that richly complex personal expression that is so distinctively characteristic of his novel: the long, tortuous, and sweeping sentence marked by parenthetical insertions and introspective disgressions, those "asides" that seem at first interruptive but actually carry the reader firmly aloft into the distant reaches of Proust's mind before bringing him safely down again when the subject ultimately finds its verb, the verb its object.

It was also at the Lycée Condorcet that the young Proust first studied philosophy under Professor Darlu, a disciple of Bergson. Darlu's concept of a reality extending far beyond the concrete world of our immediate perception was altogether compatible to this poetic-minded adolescent; the novel he would one day write deals precisely with the idea of reality as subjective rather than objective. Together with his schoolmates, Marcel organized a literary magazine and dreamed of becoming a great writer. As in *Remembrance of Things Past* (and so often in life), the boy's ambitions were not taken seriously by his father, and Proust dutifully went on to study for a career in law. Despite his asthmatic condition, he was also accepted for military service, and survived a year in the army (1889 to 1890). He seems actually to have enjoyed barracks life, and in the novel, the Narrator visits his friend Robert de St. Loup at camp, warmly recalling the affectionate camaraderie of life there.

Whether Proust engaged in homosexual practice during his school and army days is a matter of conjecture, idle conjecture at that. We do know that in 1894 he became emotionally involved with Reynaldo Hahn, destined to become a composer of minor fame, and that not long after, he transferred his feelings to Lucien Daudet, younger son of the novelist Alphonse Daudet. Both were several years younger than Proust, and both remained his lifelong friends. During that same period, he also enjoyed a brief affair with a young Englishman named Willie Heath, who met an untimely death at twenty-two. As a young man, Proust seems to have preferred lovers somewhat his junior but of his own social and intellectual station. Later in life, his interests turned toward a tougher, more virile breed.

It seems clear that the Baron de Charlus, who frequents cab drivers, workers, and male prostitutes, is at least in part a projection of Proust himself. The Baron's primary model, however, is believed to be Count Robert de Montesquiou, a poet and aesthete of Wildean proportions, to whom Proust paid court during the years 1893 to 1895. Montesquiou, like Wilde, was a flamboyant personality who took particular pleasure in shocking the bourgeoisie with decadent writing and decadent morals. As seen in letters to the Count that betray a fatuous subservience, Proust attempted to "use" him in order to gain entrance into those Parisian salons to which the latter claimed to hold the keys. In *Remembrance of Things Past,* the Baron de Charlus is portrayed as demanding just such homage, but Proust seems to take fictional revenge on the Count de Montesquiou by having the Narrator score his own social successes without the Baron's help. (In later years, it is ironic to note, the ambitious young Jean Cocteau is to be seen alternately paying court to both the aging Montesquiou and the dying Proust in his own efforts to crash Parisian literary society.)

Actually, social success came quite easily to Marcel Proust. By the time he was twenty, he found himself comfortably ensconced as a frequent guest of duchesses and countesses, hobnobbing with both the illustrious French nobility and the leading writers and artists of his day. It was a dream come true. The picture of Proust that emerges from this period may be confirmed not only by photographs but by the verbal testimony of those who knew him then. We observe a slight young man of medium height with very dark hair and sadly intense, narrow eyes, looking rather more like an eastern prince than a French bourgeois. The epithets "Persian" and "Oriental" occur frequently in descriptions of him. He seems always to have sported a mustache, and later

on a beard, which he would grow and then shave at inexplicable whim. At one point, he cultivated the affectation of a
gardenia as boutonnière, but for all his pretensions to the
role of dandy, Proust's clothes were seldom properly pressed.

His charm and intelligence made Marcel Proust a welcome and popular guest in both the literary and more
worldly salons. At first he asked nothing more than to rub
elbows with the "great," fawn on their majestic presence,
and bathe in the warmth of their splendor. Like his fictional
Narrator, however, he gradually felt the cool of disenchantment. Sensing the void into which he had ambitiously
plunged, Proust turned to writing late at night.

In 1896, he published his first book, *Les plaisirs et les
jours;* the title of the English translation, *Pleasures and Regrets,* unfortunately loses an ironic cross reference to the
Works and Days of the Greek writer Hesiod. It does, however, convey somewhat the deliquescent, hothouse quality of
Proust's book, which is a demi-decadent potpourri of
sketches, poems, and narrative tales, hardly distinguishable
in style and tone from other publications of that era. Was
Proust's father right? Was his son no more than a dabbling
dilettante? No one really seemed to take the young writer
seriously. Yet *Les plaisirs et les jours* did have an introduction by Anatole France, one of the leading literary lights of
the late nineteenth century.

Despite his being swept up in the Parisian social whirl,
Proust managed to fill an enormous quantity of notebooks
with tentative chapters of a novel about a young man named
Jean Santeuil. These pages drew heavily from his own life
and reflected an immature evaluation of his experiences in
the Faubourg St. Germain. That he did not seek to publish
this huge work does more than credit to his early but fas-
tidious critical judgment. It is proof that he had not succeeded in achieving the kind of novel which he sensed,
without yet understanding how, might encompass the more

personal expression of a vision. *Jean Santeuil,* which has
posthumously been assembled into composite and coherent
form, and published in both French and English, is a re-
spectable piece of fiction and little more. Although it is of
great interest to Proust scholars, the novel itself would surely
never have gained any lasting repute on its own merits.

In 1899, Proust immersed himself in a totally new project, retiring further from the social world. Seeking vicarious
refuge in the realm of art, he earnestly set about studying,
then translating, the work of John Ruskin whose essays on
art and architecture were then the aesthetic vogue. In these
efforts, he relied heavily on the help of a friend named
Marie Nordlinger, for Proust was not at all firmly bilingual.
He also enlisted the partial collaboration of his mother, who
knew English quite well. Within the several years following,
he had completed and published, with critical commentary,
a number of Ruskin's works including *The Bible at Amiens*
and portions of *Sesame and Lilies.*

The death of Proust's father, in December 1903, pro-
duced an unexpected effect on the son. Now thirty-four, he
still harbored an excessive attachment to his mother; he
seems, as his biographers suggest, to have hoped that his
father's death would bring his mother and him closer together. Such was not the case, for Mme. Proust clung desperately to her husband's memory, and her son found himself even further excluded. It was rather his mother's untimely
death, less than two years later, that provided a decisive
turning point in Proust's life and career. The psychological
shock of this loss and the stark realization of his solitude
bore their physical toll, and Proust was frequently under
medical care during the next few years. His brief stay, in
1905, in a sanitarium, was exaggerated for fictional purposes
into the Narrator's lengthy internment. Gradually, he returned to health, to society, and to himself. It was this new

and overwhelming sense of liberation, as he learned to accept his parents' deaths, that finally enabled him, virtually a middle-aged man, to realize himself more openly as the homosexual that he was, and more freely as the writer of genius that he was.

The discipline of his long literary apprenticeship soon bore double fruit. The study of Ruskin had introduced him to a world more permanent and meaningful than that of the Faubourg. At the same time, his mind was teeming with anecdotes and sketches of the people he had known and studied. While sharpening his critical faculties in the timeless world of art, he had not lost the urge to create fiction. He had also acquired the regular habit of writing, without which one's creative fire goes up in smoke like so many wasted hours of salon life.

Sometime during 1908, Proust conceived a most curious and unorthodox literary project, which was to be part criticism, part fiction. For a dozen years or so, he had been an occasional contributor to *Le Figaro,* the leading Parisian newspaper, submitting social and literary articles, satirical pieces and personal recollections. As the premise for his new book, Proust imagined the situation of a writer who is awaiting publication of an article sent to *Le Figaro.* His mother, ripe for exorcising, appears as a character; drawing from actual memory, he constructs a series of dialogues between mother and son, interpolated with essays on writers and theories of literature. In effect, foreshadowing the Narrator of *Remembrance of Things Past,* Proust is here developing (though in tentative and primitive form), those ideas on art and artists, and the artistic vision as a means of grasping life, that will eventually give shape and substance to his own great novel. It is significant, too, that Proust now took the giant creative step from third-person narration, which presumes the author's distance and detachment, and which had proved a barrier to his full creative expression in *Jean San-teuil*, to the free and unlimited horizons of the personal "I."

Like *Jean Santeuil*, these random critical pieces and reminiscences, including sketchy portraits of the Guerman-tes and other characters, have been collected and published. The title, *Contre Sainte-Beuve*, refers to the nineteenth-century critic whose theories and methodology had held sway for almost a hundred years and which, despite Proust's skillful attack, have not entirely disappeared.* It was Sainte-Beuve's contention that a knowledge of any writer's personal life is indispensable to a full understanding of his work; the more we know about the man, the better equipped we are to penetrate and interpret his art. Proust advanced the dia-metrically opposite view, that the man and the artist are separate beings, that the writer virtually becomes another when he recreates experience in terms of fiction or poetry. Proust, we have noted time and again, held that from life, from so-called reality, the artist draws freely, abundantly, necessarily. But for him it is the transformation of reality rather than its literal reproduction that produces art and in turn endows experience with meaning. What the writer should seek to reproduce—what Marcel Proust himself sought—are not the sights, sounds, and events of actual experience but the more permanently poetic, time-transcend-ing distillation of those sights, sounds, and events that com-pose our material experience, recaptured through the meta-morphosis of memory and refashioned as the personal myth of fiction.

Having failed as a writer of fiction in *Jean Santeuil*, Proust found the key to his future novel, *Remembrance of*

* In English, *On Art and Literature*. The central incident of the writer awaiting the appearance of his article is retained and mentioned sporadically in *Remembrance of Things Past*.

Things Past, by first evolving its underlying ideas in the form of critical literary theory. One of the first sentences in his *Contre Sainte-Beuve* provides the all-important, quasi-mystical clue: "What our intelligence recognizes as our past life is not really that past at all. . . . Every hour of our lives, once gone, becomes incarnate in some material object where it remains captive until such time as we discover and recognize that object." In *Swann's Way,* he recapitulates the notion of buried memories awaiting reincarnation, and in *The Past Recaptured,* we find this variation on a theme: "An hour is not merely an hour of time, it is a vase filled with perfumes and sounds, atmospheres and dreams." For Proust, the writer neither records nor invents, he discovers and *translates;* in so doing, he communicates a vision whereby each of us may perhaps discover and translate his own life.

From 1909 until his death in 1922, Marcel Proust devoted himself with the fanaticism of a religious ascetic to writing the seven volumes of his novel. He had lived enough in this world and he knew it. He was beginning to die, and he knew that also. And so, at thirty-eight, he withdrew almost entirely from the vain social existence he had once so coveted and prized, becoming a virtual recluse in order to translate the chronicle of his experience. To finish his book was to become a race against time and death, just as a key theme of the novel itself is man's struggle against time and death.

Recluse is perhaps too forbidding a word, for it was in the last dozen years of his life, paradoxically, that he also became known as "Proust of the Ritz." By way of contrast with his routine anchorite existence—propped up in bed in a hot, dry room, partaking indifferently of food, writing for hours on end—Proust would occasionally sally forth at midnight to meet friends after the theater. He would appear in the swankiest of hotels, looking like a crumpled clown, swathed in an out-sized fur coat (no matter what the season or the temperature), consuming only iced beer or orange-ade, while hosting the most lavish of supper parties. Although such ventures into the Parisian night were not that frequent, they were sufficiently eccentric to become legendary. Except for summer stays on the Norman seacoast, brief or protracted, depending on his health, Proust remained hermitlike—indeed almost hermetically sealed—within the four walls of his bedroom, which he had had lined with cork as a sound barrier.

Such poses and gestures were not self-conscious eccentricity; as Proust's asthma and nervous condition worsened, he became increasingly more unstable. He lived an almost exclusively nocturnal existence, going to sleep at dawn. In the middle of the night he would dispatch notes to indulgent friends inquiring about a matter of art, history, or royal protocol; he would expect, and generally got, an answer. He could then go on writing, although he might well distort the factual information thus received. On at least one occasion, he was overcome with the desire to hear a particular piece of chamber music and summoned an astonished but well-compensated string quartet to play for him in private in the small hours of the morning, while he gulped a plate of cold noodles. He would then proceed to record his impressions on paper. The Proust of these years was a far cry from the dandy of 1891, photographed strumming a tennis racquet as though it were a banjo.

A handful of privileged friends was permitted access to Proust's cork-lined cell; Cocteau, one of that company, was among the few to read the manuscript of *Remembrance of Things Past*. Yet Proust's only regular companions were his servants, who guarded the master's privacy against unwelcome intruders and who catered unquestioningly to his whims and eccentricities. The choice of one of these servants was to change the course of his life and work.

It was early in 1913, as Proust readied his first volume

for publication, that he rehired a young man named Alfred Agostinelli, who had served as his chauffeur during the summer of 1907. The exact nature of their relationship remains clothed in mystery. Since he seldom went out, he had little need for a chauffeur; and Agostinelli now had a wife, who entered Proust's service as a housekeeper. It is generally believed, whether sex was involved or not, that Proust desperately attempted to make Alfred exclusively *his,* a personal possession in the prison of his apartment. The young man soon ran off and was killed while learning to fly a plane the following spring. The intensity of emotions Proust experienced, ranging from love and desire to sorrow and the tortures of the damned, so left their mark that his original project for a novel was increased by several volumes. While it is grossly inexact to think of the Narrator's Albertine as merely Alfred Agostinelli given a girl's name, there is little doubt that Proust's experience with the dark stranger from Monaco gave greater depths to his pages on love and jealousy, as well as greatly swelling their number.

The reception accorded the appearance of *Du côté de chez Swann* (*Swann's Way*) in the fall of 1913, was modest and mixed. Proust was simultaneously assailed for his unorthodox, discursive style and acclaimed for the poetry of his language and his vision. Yet virtually no one, save a handful of Proust's intimates, could even suspect what heights this complex, leisurely narrative was eventually destined to reach.

The manuscript had been summarily rejected by a popular publishing house as well as by the young, more artistic-minded *Nouvelle Revue Française*. It was indeed his fellow novelist André Gide who made the official rejection. Proust was reduced to having his first volume printed at his own expense. Now the critical flurry attendant upon the work caused the *Nouvelle Revue Française* to reconsider and editor André Gide to apologize. Repenting his earlier indiscretion, he invited Proust to publish succeeding volumes with his firm.

After considerable legal and financial dickering—and the untoward advent of a world war—Proust's second volume was brought out by *NRF* in June 1919, together with the reissue of *Swann's Way*. *A l'ombre des jeunes filles en fleurs* (*Within a Budding Grove*) was at first less successful than its predecessor, but when the new work was awarded the prestigious Goncourt Prize, Proust's success as a writer was secure. He proved to be a publisher's nemesis, however, not only making minor corrections and additions as he read proofs, but developing entire new sections for his work. Once he had totally conceived the sweep of the book, Proust would draft unanticipated new narrative segments, and then return to earlier portions where he would subtly interject "beacons," planting the seeds of events to follow. But the editors at *NRF* were wise enough to let Proust be Proust.

When he ceased to be, on 18 November 1922, he was still feverishly writing, rewriting, editing. According to Proustian legend, the last passage he dictated was a revision of the death of Bergotte: the visit to the museum, the "little patch of yellow," the light in the window. But the final volume, *Le temps retrouvé*, had for the most part been long since composed, for the moment when Proust began writing his novel was the moment when time had been recaptured.

The novel he projected in 1909 was to be in three parts, roughly corresponding to what we now know as *Swann's Way, The Guermantes Way,* and *The Past Recaptured*. While Proust did not thoroughly foresee all the characters nor all the events that would so greatly expand his initial scheme, the overall design was clearly envisioned and solidly conceived in terms of structure.

His book was to be the life of a writer and would narrate the evolution of that writer's vocation. It would focus on the social world he knew most intimately and would describe that world in progressive terms of dream, reality, and disenchantment—reflecting precisely the stages of his own emotional involvement with the Faubourg St. Germain. Proust's novel, and the novel that implicitly germinates within its framework, would embody and demonstrate a philosophy of life, a vision, an aesthetic, a veritable metaphysics of being. He wanted to show how habit and convention, conformity and prejudice—our automatic, mechanistic reflexes to experience—blind us to ulterior reality. At the end of a century of progressive scientific awakening and the dawn of a miraculous new era whose monstrous machinery could not even be imagined, Proust opted for the greater, more complex miracle of man's psyche. He saw in those human instruments, regenerative memory and creative imagination, the necessary equipment for self-understanding; he saw the vital direction of man's individual realization not to be relentlessly forward but meaningfully backward, embracing our recovered past.

So it is, on completing *Remembrance of Things Past,* that we find ourselves in the simple, yet in some ways perplexing, position of just having read about an author who is about to write a novel—which is the story of his life and how he came to write that novel. We, together with the novelist, have come full cycle. However, most critics to the contrary, the book does not actually form a full and perfect circle, as Germaine Breé has astutely pointed out in her excellent study, *Marcel Proust and Deliverance from Time.* The opening segments of the novel are, in point of fact, prefatory fragments in a kind of limbo, not literally outside time but certainly outside the circular sweep the novel seems ultimately to describe.

Although the reader cannot realize it, on opening *Swann's Way* for the first time, the awakening Narrator is at Tansonville, visiting Gilberte de St. Loup, half dreaming, half reminiscing—a scene not pictured in detail until early in the final volume. His recollections of Combray are either dim or artificial, stimulated only by the intellect, until the incident of the *madeleine*, at some later date, recaptures the true memories in present, extradimensional vividness. The novel itself, like the town of Combray, then springs forth from that cup of sensory impressions. Whether we, like Marcel, will enjoy such privileged moments of *mémoire involontaire* is less important than the lesson we may derive from his example: the liberation and surrender of our senses to the validity of experience, the readiness to acknowledge its pattern and meaning. Does each of us not live the novel of his own life?

Readers of fiction have come to expect the author to account for what happens finally to his characters. Proust's originality lies not in the rather trumped-up device of reuniting his cast in the "masked ball" scene, but rather in its ironic twist. We find it does not matter what has become of them, but what becomes of him: how he incorporates all their successive selves into the unifying entity of his own life, a process of self-realization.

That masterful ending takes on still more vital meaning when contrasted with a Henry James work of like philosophical orientation. In *The Beast in the Jungle,* one of James's most disturbing tales, a man spends his life waiting, literally wastes that life in expectation of what he believes is destined to happen to him. The terrifying thing, the "beast" that stalks, is that nothing whatsoever was destined to happen. Proust makes the opposite demonstration: a life seems wasted and empty, irretrievably consumed by time, when a revelation of the mind, a dramatic pivoting of viewpoint, transforms his whole existence in retrospect. Nothing past has altered; it is the writer's awakened faculties of vision and interpretation that uncover and enlighten the "hidden" meaning.

As previously noted, Proust's monumental community of characters are all fictional creations, though composites of real men and women who walked among the worlds he knew. There is more than one model for Gilberte and Odette, the Duc and Duchesse de Guermantes, just as several household servants contributed to the making of Françoise. Swann and the Baron de Charlus are not without their real-life counterparts, but there is as much of Marcel Proust in these two memorable personages as in the fictional Narrator. They form a kind of tripartite. Swann, a potential artist, partakes too much of life and dies a dilettante, unfulfilled. His death coincides with the ascendance of Charlus as an increasingly major character who, in his own way, follows Swann's way. It is their common destiny to transcend the bonds of time only through memorialization by the Narrator who makes them part of his book.

The events of *Remembrance of Things Past* largely reflect the experience of Marcel Proust, his own life transformed primarily in terms of an inner, near spiritual experience. The Christian, heterosexual Narrator is a more universal "hero" than the writer Marcel Proust. While the factor of psychological sublimation is probably a valid one as well, the transcription of Proust's own ethnic origins and sexual orientation would have deflected the reader's focus from the key theme of the novel.

Another factor in determining the Narrator's identity may well have been the celebrated Dreyfus Affair. When, in 1894, a Jewish army officer was falsely accused of treason, France was split into two camps for a dozen years. As the Dreyfus case is frequently debated in Proust's novel, the Narrator is able to maintain a kind of objectivity. Actually, Proust's own pro-Dreyfus stand does show through, for the various anti-Dreyfusards are portrayed as prejudiced fools. By the same token, the Duc de Guermantes is persuaded by a simple, logical argument of the officer's innocence, whereas Swann, a Jew, defends Dreyfus out of emotional blindness.

The factor of homosexuality was at least equally sensitive for Proust, and still more personal. Aside from the tenor of the times, so different from our own, one may conjecture that Marcel Proust had for so long concealed his sexual life from his parents while they were living, that he was unable to "free" himself even in fiction after their death. Artistic dictates, however, seem more valid. Proust was clearly quite knowledgeable about the world he calls Sodom and Gomorrah, but here again he wished to preserve his creative objectivity as well as his identity. He had no desire—like Gide who, perhaps hypocritically, was "shocked" by parts of Proust's novel—to confess or undertake a personalized study of inversion, no desire to expose or to champion a cause.

Proust depicted the world of homosexuality as one of several that he knew, juxtaposing its mores with those of the Faubourg world as yet another universe of masks and protocol. The Narrator also makes clear, in *The Past Recaptured,* that the "laws" of love seem particularly magnified when observed in homosexuals. The critique of Proust's increasing obsession with homosexuality in *Remembrance of Things Past* seems justifiable, but one must bear in mind that during the writing of his later volumes, he was a dying man, in many ways obsessed. Nor did he live to complete the editing of those volumes.

It is wrong, however, as most Proust commentators now agree, to suppose that the women in the novel are somehow mere transpositions of men. Proust understood the feminine mystique well; his female characters, for the most part, are incontestably authentic. The long-standing notion that Albertine (a name no more masculine than the common girl's name Gilberte, which it resembles) was a fictional projection of the chauffeur Agostinelli, has been discredited.

Prior to the Agostinelli affair, Proust had already evolved his dark view of love as debilitating rather than exhilarating, love as a subjective illusion that makes of us prisoners. He had composed the episode of *Swann in Love,* which outlines the mechanisms of his psychological theories. There is nothing homosexual in Swann's fatal infatuation with Odette, and this is the affair that serves as a model for Proustian love. The Albertine episode is no more than an intensification of emotional states Proust had already studied.

One thing is certain, however. Proust's personal drama with his chauffeur-secretary left a terrible scar, particularly the effect of Agostinelli's untimely death. From that experience, emerged the two extraordinary volumes not originally envisioned by Proust. One of Albertine's great "mysteries" is indeed her "otherness," her alleged lesbianism. It has been suggested that this is the equivalent of Agostinelli's "otherness," his heterosexuality. The psychological question Proust is exploring, however, is more general than its particular model; frustration in the face of unattainability is a universal experience. If Proust's ideas and his characters were insufficiently universal, his novel would not have survived, ever increasing in prestige. We need not be mad to understand Lear's madness, nor do most men murder when experiencing Othello's jealousy, yet we respond with empathy to such emotional states.

Proust's universality has been impugned by occasional critics and readers in terms of the novel's alleged snobbery. It is, on the contrary, the very universality of snobbery that fascinates Proust. He observes it at every level of society, mocks it and punctures its pompousness. As a very young man, Marcel Proust may have affected a snobbish tone himself; his novel is filled with recurrent attacks on the folly and viciousness of *snobisme* in every form. No understanding reader can misinterpret the nature of the Narrator's infatuation with the Duchesse. It is the legend that he venerates, not the reality, and surely, not for long, the society of the Faubourg St. Germain.

Long after the dream has lost its enchantment, though, there lingers in the air a faint trace of nostalgia for the magic of the historic, near mythic name Guermantes: the incarnation of an ideal, the poetry of the sound, the symbolic durability of the towering aged Duc as man in history, man in time, less nobleman than noble man. This is not snobbery but the poetry of faith.

Proust's retreat from the world, at the age of thirty-eight, offers a curious parallel in literary history. It was on his thirty-eighth birthday that Michel de Montaigne, the father of modern French literature, declaring himself weary of society, took to the tower of his castle. There he read, meditated on life's experience, and finally poured forth his thoughts, boldly defying tradition by expressing them in terms of the personal "I." These were the first philosophic essays in modern French.

In the cell-like confines of his cork-lined room, Marcel Proust gave his life to completing what may be the definitive novel, the crowning achievement of a form. For its inordinate length, *Remembrance of Things Past* boasts precious little "plot." Read like Dante or Milton, as a majestic poem, the novel bursts the seams of its historical social setting and emerges as a new mythology. The characters, for all their admixture of vice and virtue, strength and weakness—indeed because of that admixture—stride boldly into our memory with Olympian authority. The work becomes, too, a philosophic epic as the Narrator pursues the sacred revelation of his own life.

Small imperfections—here lacks, there excesses—mar the pure, probably unattainable, artistic perfection for which an artist strives. More than a work of art, however, Marcel

Proust's novel was for him an act of self-discovery and redemption. In an analogy to those Arabian "thousand and one nights" of which Proust was so fond, critic J.-P. Richard observes that, like Scheherazade, the author of *Remembrance of Things Past* is telling his tale in order to save his life.

Proust's personal predilection for three very different books—*The Mémoires of St. Simon,* Balzac's *Comédie Humaine,* and the *Arabian Nights*—tells us much about the kind of work he set out to create himself. Today's readers and critics, with the distance of time, can now view Proust the novelist in the light of two other perspectives: as the heir of certain French literary traditions with which he was deeply familiar, and as a twentieth-century writer sharing with contemporaries whose work he did not know, an anxious awareness of man's role as a solitary stranger in the universe.

If Proust rejected one literary current of his time, fiercely realistic naturalism, it was to explore the nature of subjective reality, as advocated by theorists of symbolism. Within *Remembrance of Things Past,* there are also frequent references to Baudelaire, whose sonnet "Correspondences" had suggested a world of wonders undiscovered in the visible universe and influenced the evolution of symbolist literature.

As a psychological novel, *Remembrance of Things Past* has roots even deeper in tradition. Detailed analysis of human emotions and the intellectualization of love have long been preoccupations of the French spirit, generally accompanied by an axiomatic cynicism. *La Princesse de Clèves,* in 1678, is considered the first in a long line of "modern" novels that explore in infinite detail the ravages of the human heart. Two eighteenth-century novels further pursued this analytical technique: *Manon Lescaut,* in which jealous rage destroys a man in love, and *Les liaisons dangereuses,* wherein cold calculation rather than sentiment controls the motivations of lovers.

More recent literary ancestors in this tradition were
Benjamin Constant, whose *Adolphe,* in 1816, delineated the
frustrations of a man trapped in the illusions of love, and
Stendhal whose 1830 novel, *Le rouge et le noir,* stands as a
model of incisive psychological analysis. When Proust wrote
"Suffering tells us more about psychology than does psychology itself," he was not only stating what he himself had
learned of love, but acknowledging the accumulated wisdom
of his predecessors in examining the mechanics of behavior.
But Proust was a moralist as well. *Remembrance of Things
Past* is filled with just such maxims, reminiscent of the sev-
enteenth-century *Maximes* of La Rochefoucauld. Proust,
who once called pessimism "our daily bread," seems generally to share La Rochefoucauld's cynical view of man as
proud, selfish, foolish . . . and solitary.

Yet for Proust there is the light in the window. Not
only the book that he felt had redeemed his own lost life,
but a glimmer of hope that we may discover and embrace
redemptive meaning in our own lives. In this, he seems to
echo the very first of the French philosophic writers, the
Renaissance essayist Montaigne. In one of his last essays,
On Experience, Montaigne chides the foolishness of men
who despair of the idleness of their lives or even the apparently uneventful emptiness of a single day. "What! Have you
not at least lived?" asks Montaigne. "That is not only the
most basic but the most illustrious of your occupations." If
we have given some measure of meditation to the meaning
and pattern of our existence, somehow managed to "ar-
range" our life and can acknowledge it as *ours,* without
nurturing a hollow illusion of what might have been, we
have, Montaigne believes, performed "the greatest task of
all."

It is not unreasonable, I believe, to recognize here a
distant glimmer of what Proust implicitly formulates as a

beacon for guiding the lives of those of us not destined to become artists. If *Remembrance of Things Past* were no more than a "remembrance" it would nonetheless take its place among the world's great novels for stylistic power, imposing characterizations, and social documentation. If Proust's work were only a hymn to art and a catechism for the artist, its universality would be considerably diminished. Beyond both these levels, it is the metaphysical ingredient— the possibility of extratemporal reality—that gives the novel its distinctively Proustian stamp. Even as a boy in Combray, Marcel narrates that the book he dreams of writing would have a "philosophical subject." This is not explained. Neither he nor his creator comes to grips with the taunting problem of man in time until much later in life.

Proust was not alone among his contemporaries in seeking new ways for the serious artist to cope with the challenge of time, the dilemma of time absolute versus time relative. In *The Magic Mountain,* Thomas Mann supposed a world outside the reaches of time. Both Faulkner and Virginia Woolf, in different ways, forced their readers to grapple with temporal sequences consciously defiant of conventional chronology. Memory and inner vision, as in Proust, transcend time. In *Ulysses,* James Joyce made the bold experiment of compressing entire lives into the confines of a single day, creating a universe under the light of eternity within the twenty-four hours of a Dublin clock.

Among Gertrude Stein's many tantalizing paradoxes, we find these lines: "We cannot retrace our steps, going forward may be the same as going backwards." T. S. Eliot, in his ultimate poetic testament *Four Quartets,* stated: "In my beginning is my end . . . In my end is my beginning . . . What we call the beginning is often the end/And to make an end is to make a beginning." Proust's hard-won but essential optimism is apparent if we contrast his philosophic position with that of his American contemporary Thomas Wolfe who first "looked homeward," then concluded, "you can't go home again."

For Proust, Combray is the only place to which we can, and must, turn. It is there that we discover the man in the child, the child in the man, and recognize that they are one. Proust's crystallized reflection on life, if one may venture to extract the quintessence of so vast a work as *Remembrance of Things Past,* seems not far distant from that of Eliot in the *Little Gidding* movement of *Four Quartets:*

> We shall not cease from exploration
> And the end of all our exploring
> Will be to arrive where we started
> And know the place for the first time.

Bibliography

1. Works by Marcel Proust

Les plaisirs et les jours. Paris: Calmann Lévy, 1896. —*Pleasures and Regrets*. Translated by Louise Varèse. New York: Crown, 1948.

Du côté de chez Swann. Paris: Bernard Grasset, 1913. —*Swann's Way*. Translated by C. K. Scott Moncrief. New York: T. Seltzer, 1924.

A l'ombre des jeunes filles en fleurs. Paris: NRF/Gallimard, 1918. —*Within a Budding Grove*. Translated by C. K. Scott Moncrief. New York: T. Seltzer, 1924.

Pastiches et mélanges. Paris: NRF/Gallimard, 1921.

Le côté de Guermantes. Paris: NRF/Gallimard, 1920–21. —*The Guermantes Way*. Translated by C. K. Scott Moncrief. New York: T. Seltzer, 1925.

Sodome et Gomorrhe. Paris: NRF/Gallimard, 1921–22. —*Cities of the Plain*. Translated by C. K. Scott Moncrief. New York: T. Seltzer, 1927.

La prisonnière. Paris: NRF/Gallimard, 1923. —*The Captive*. Translated by C. K. Scott Moncrief. New York: Modern Library, 1929.

Albertine disparue (La fugitive). Paris: NRF/Gallimard, 1925.
    —*The Sweet Cheat Gone*. Translated by C. K. Scott Mon-
    crief. New York: Modern Library, 1930.
Le temps retrouvé. Paris: NRF/Gallimard, 1927. —*The Past
    Recaptured*. Translated by Frederick A. Blossom. New York:
    A. & C. Boni, 1932.
Chroniques. Paris: NRF/Gallimard, 1927.
Jean Santeuil. Paris: Gallimard, 1952. —*Jean Santeuil*. Translated
    by Gerard Hopkins. New York: Simon and Schuster, 1956.
Contre Sainte-Beuve. Paris: Gallimard, 1954. —*On Art and Lit-
    erature*. Translated by Sylvia Townsend Warner. New York:
    Meridian Books, 1958.

2. *A Selection of Books in English about Marcel Proust*

Ames, V. M. *Proust and Santayana: The Aesthetic Way of Life*.
    Chicago: Willett, Clark, 1937.

Beckett, Samuel. *Proust*. New York: Grove Press, 1957.

Bersani, Leo. *Marcel Proust: The Fictions of Life and Art*. New
    York: Oxford University Press, 1965.

Brée, Germaine. *Marcel Proust and Deliverance from Time*. New
    Brunswick, N. J.: Rutgers University Press, 1969.

Coleman, Elliott. *The Golden Angel: Papers on Proust*. New
    York: Coley Taylor, 1954.

Deleuze, Gilles. *Proust and Signs*. New York: Braziller, 1972.

Girard, René, ed. *Proust: A Collection of Critical Essays*. Engle-
    wood Cliffs, N. J.: Prentice-Hall, 1962.

Graham, Victor E. *The Imagery of Proust*. Oxford: Blackwell,
    1966.

Green, F. C. *The Mind of Proust: A Detailed Interpretation of
    "A la recherche du temps perdu."* Cambridge: Cambridge
    University Press, 1949.

Jephcott, E. F. *Proust and Rilke: The Literature of Expanded
    Consciousness*. London: Chatto & Windus, 1972.

Kopp, Richard L. *Marcel Proust as a Social Critic*. Rutherford,
    N. J.: Fairleigh Dickinson University Press, 1971.

Maurois, André. *Proust: Portrait of a Genius*. New York: Harper, 1950.

Moss, Howard. *The Magic Lantern of Marcel Proust*. New York: Macmillan, 1962.

Painter, George. *Proust: The Early Years/The Later Years*. 2 vols. New York: Atlantic-Little, Brown, 1959–65.

Quennell, Peter, ed. *Marcel Proust 1871–1922: A Centennial Volume*. New York: Simon and Schuster, 1971.

Revel, Jean-François. *On Proust*. New York: Library Press, 1972.

Sansom, William. *Proust and His World*. New York: Scribner, 1974.

Shattuck, Roger. *Proust's Binoculars: A Study of Memory, Time and Recognition in "A la recherche du temps perdu."* New York: Random House, 1963.

Wolitz, Seth L. *The Proustian Community*. New York: New York University Press, 1971.

3. *A Selection of Articles in English about Marcel Proust*

Auchincloss, Louis. "Proust's Picture of Society." *Partisan Review*, No. 27 (1960), pp. 690–701.

Cocking, John M. "Proust and Painting." In *French Nineteenth-Century Painting and Literature*. Manchester: Manchester University Press, 1972.

Collin, P. H. "Food and Drink in *A la recherche du temps perdu.*" *Neophilologus*, No. 54 (1970), pp. 244–257.

Ellis, Havelock. "In Search of Proust." In *From Rousseau to Proust*. New York: Houghton Mifflin, 1935.

Genette, Gérard. "Time and Narrative in *A la recherche du temps perdu.*" In *Aspects of Narrative*. Edited by J. Hillis Miller. New York: Columbia University Press, 1971.

Houston, John Porter. *Fictional Techniques in France, 1802–1927*. Baton Rouge: Louisiana State University Press, 1972.

Krutch, Joseph Wood. "Marcel Proust." In *Five Masters: A Study in the Mutations of the Novel*. Gloucester, Mass.: Peter Smith, 1968.

Levin, Harry. "Proust." In *The Gates of Horn: A Study of Five French Realists*. New York: Oxford University Press, 1963.

———. "Proust, Gide, and the Sexes." In *Grounds for Comparison*. Cambridge, Mass.: Harvard University Press, 1972.

Meyers, Jeffrey. "Proust's Aesthetic Analogies: Character and Painting in Swann's Way." *Journal of Aesthetics and Art Criticism,* No. 30 (1972), pp. 377–88.

O'Brien, Justin. "Involuntary Memory before Proust." In *Contemporary French Literature*. New Brunswick, N. J.: Rutgers University Press, 1971.

———. "Marcel Proust as a *Moraliste*." *Romantic Review*, No. 38 (1948), pp. 50–69.

Poulet, Georges. "Proust." In *Studies in Human Time*. New York: Harper and Row (Torchback), 1956.

Price, Larkin B. "Bird Imagery Surrounding Proust's Albertine." *Symposium*, No. 26 (1972), pp. 242–60.

Robertson, Jane. "The Relationship Between the Hero and Françoise." *French Studies*, No. 25 (1971), pp. 437–41.

Turquet-Milnes, G. "Marcel Proust." In *From Pascal to Proust*. New York: Boni & Liveright, 1926.

Ullman, Stephen. "The Writer and His Tools: Proust's Views on Language and Style in His Letters to His Critics." In *History and Structure of French: Essays in Honor of T. B. W. Reid*. Totowa, N. J.: Rowan & Littlefield, 1972.

Weitz, Morris. *Philosophy in Literature: Shakespeare, Voltaire, Tolstoy and Proust*. Detroit: Wayne State University Press, 1963.

Wilson, Edmund. "Marcel Proust." In *Axel's Castle*. New York: Scribner's, 1931.

Index

Adolphe (Constant), 110
aesthetics, 24, 75, 77–80
Agostinelli, Alfred, 101, 106–107
A la recherche du temps perdu. See: Remembrance of Things Past
Albertine, 15–17, 24, 33, 41–49, 53–54, 59–60, 71–72, 78, 84, 86, 90, 101, 106–107
A l'ombre des jeunes filles en fleurs. See: Within a Budding Grove
Andrée, 46
Arabian Nights, 8, 109
art
  love and, 11, 75
  Proust's concept of, 66, 75, 77, 79, 81, 88, 90, 97
  Swann and, 24, 37–38
artists in *Remembrance of Things Past. See:* Bergotte; Elstir; Vinteuil

Balbec, 12, 14–17, 23–25, 29, 31–32, 41–42, 45, 48–49, 64, 71, 76, 78, 87
  church at, 13, 79
Balzac, Honoré de, 7, 49, 109
Baron, the. *See:* Charlus
Baudelaire, Charles, 82, 109
Bellini, Gentile, 38
Bergotte, 11, 24, 65, 74–78, 84–87
Bergson, Henri, 78, 93
Bible, the, 22, 82–83
Bible at Amiens, The (Ruskin), 96
Botticelli, Sandro, 37
Brée, Germaine, 103

Captive, The, 41, 44
   episodes of, 44–46
Champs-Elysées, 39, 59,
   61, 65
Charlus, Baron de, 17–18,
   22–24, 33, 48–52, 58,
   60–62, 68–69, 71, 74,
   83–85, 87, 94, 105
Chartres, 2
Châtellerault, Duc de, 23,
   66
Cities of the Plain, 22, 25,
   49, 83
   episodes of, 22–23, 49–50
Cocteau, Jean, 94, 100
Combray, 2, 9–10, 12–13,
   16, 18–19, 23–25, 29,
   32, 38–39, 42, 48, 57–
   58, 67, 71–72, 74, 84,
   86–87, 91, 104, 111–
   12
Comédie Humaine, La
   (Balzac), 7, 49, 109
Constant, Benjamin, 110
Contre Sainte-Beuve, 98–99
côté de Guermantes, Le.
   See: Guermantes
   Way, The
Cottard, Dr., 43
cubism, 78

Dante, 108
Daudet, Alphonse, 93
Daudet, Lucien, 93
death, as a theme, 6, 22,

   67–68, 85, 87, 99
Dickens, Charles, 35
Dreyfus Affair, the, 105–
   106
Duchesse, the. *See:* Guer-
   mantes
Du côté de chez Swann.
   See: Swann's Way

Eliot, T. S., 111–12
Elstir, 15, 24, 74, 76–79, 84

Faubourg St. Germain, 3,
   18–19, 23–24, 34, 41,
   50, 85, 103, 108
Faulkner, William, 111
Fauré, Gabriel, 78
Figaro, Le (newspaper), 97
Flaubert, Gustave, 3
Forcheville, Mme. de
   (Odette), 30, 69.
   See also: Odette
Four Quartets (Eliot), 111–
   12
France, Anatole, 78, 95
Franck, César, 78
Françoise, 9, 40, 46, 84–85
Franco-Prussian War, 91
Freud, Sigmund, 28
Fugitive, La. See: Sweet
   Cheat Gone, The

Galsworthy, John, 4
Geneviève de Brabant, 12
Gide, André, 101, 106

Gilberte, 11, 13, 24, 29–30,
33, 39–43, 48, 53–54,
56–60, 65, 67–68, 70,
74–75, 87, 103, 106
Giotto, 11
Gomorrah, 22, 23, 25, 44,
50, 75, 106
grandmother, the Narrator's,
16–17, 29, 65

Guermantes, Duc de, 18–21,
50, 69, 85, 105, 108
Guermantes, Duchesse de,
12–14, 16, 18–21, 24,
30, 33, 43, 46, 54,
68–71, 108
Guermantes, Prince de, 69
Guermantes, Princesse de,
19, 61
Mme. Verdurin becomes,
69–70
Guermantes family, the,
16–17, 20–22, 53, 85,
108
Guermantes Way, The, 102
episodes of, 17–22
"Guermantes Way, the" (as
path and metaphor),
10, 50, 57, 71

habit, as a theme, 9, 32–34,
40, 47, 103
Hahn, Reynaldo, 93
Hesiod, 95

homosexuality, as a theme,
22–23, 33, 48–49, 52–
53, 58, 84, 92–93, 106
humanism, 82

Illiers, 2, 91
illusion, as a theme, 12, 14,
20, 23–25, 30, 36–37,
45–47, 52, 54, 75, 80,
82, 107
impressionism, 78
interior monologue, 6
"intermittences of the heart,"
Proust's theory of, 30,
33, 48

James, Henry, 104
jealousy, as a theme, 36, 38,
40, 43, 51, 53, 101
Jean Santeuil, 95–97
Joyce, James, 6, 111
Jupien, 49–50, 52, 61, 87

Kafka, Franz, 36, 48

Lady in Pink, the (Odette),
30, 58
Lady in White, the (Odette),
39, 58, 72
La Rochefoucauld, Duc de,
110
Léonie, Aunt, 9–10, 14, 24,
84, 86
lesbianism, 22, 37, 43, 46,
74, 77, 107

liaisons dangereuses, Les
        (Choderlos de Lac-
        los), 109
Louis XIV, 8
love, as a theme, 11, 33, 37,
        40, 44–45, 54, 75, 107

madeleine, incident of the,
        8, 28, 38, 63, 104
magic lantern, 12, 20, 25,
        32, 67, 72, 86
Magic Mountain, The
        (Mann), 111
Mann, Thomas, 111
Manon Lescaut (Prévost
        d'Exiles), 109
"Marcel," as the Narrator's
        own name, 5, 90
*Marcel Proust and Deliver-
        ance from Time*
        (Brée), 103
Marquise, the. *See:* Ville-
        parisis
McCullers, Carson, 15
Mélusine, 20
memory, as a theme, 6, 8, 13,
        25, 28, 30, 67–68, 98,
        111
    and *mémoire involontaire*,
        28, 31, 38, 62, 64,
        104. *See also: made-
        leine*
Méséglise, 10
Milton, John, 108
Molière, 36

Montaigne, 108, 110
Montesquiou, Count Robert
        de, 94
Morel, "Charlie," 33, 50–51,
        71, 74, 84
mother's good-night kiss, as
        a theme, 10–11, 16,
        42, 46
Musset, Alfred de, 35

Narrator, the
    Albertine and, 15–16, 33,
        41–48
    at Balbec, 12–17, 30–33,
        41, 76, 78
    childhood at Combray, 9–
        12
    the Duchesse and, 12,
        18–20, 30, 33
    Gilberte and, 11, 33, 39–41,
        48, 57–60
    identity of, 4–6, 66, 90–91,
        105–106
    and the novel he will
        write, 24, 66, 71–72,
        84, 90, 111
    at a sanitarium, 60
naturalism, 7
Nouvelle Revue Française
        (NRF publishing
        house), 101–102

Odette (Mme. Swann), 10,
        29–30, 33–38, 41–42,
        44, 48, 50, 58, 67, 69,
        71, 76, 87

On Art and Literature, 98n
O'Neill, Eugene, 82
Opéra, episode at the, 19–20, 66

Painter, George D., 4
Past Recaptured, The, 8, 28, 56, 70–71, 79, 86, 99, 102, 107
episodes of, 57–71
Pleasures and Regrets, 95
Princesse de Clèves, La, 109
prisoner, as a theme, 10, 15, 22, 39, 47, 51, 87, 101, 107
Prisonnière, La. See: Captive, The
Proust, Dr. Adrien (father), 91, 93, 96
Proust, Mme. (mother), 91–92, 96–97
Proust, Marcel
in army service, 93
asthma, suffers from, 91, 93, 100
centenary of, 2
death of, 90, 99, 102
early writings of, 93, 95–98
early years of, 91–94
French literary tradition, his place in, 6–7, 109–111
wins Goncourt Prize, 102

homosexual problems of, 93–94, 97, 101, 106
publication difficulties of, 101–102
society, enters, 94–95; retires from, 99–100, 108
Proust, Robert (brother), 91–92
Proust family, the, 2, 91
psychology
"great laws" of, 28, 32–33, 36
of love, 35–37, 42–43, 46
Proust as psychologist, 8, 23, 47, 86, 107, 109
See also: habit; illusion; "intermittences of the heart"; memory; "successive selves"

Queen of Naples, 51, 62, 83

Rachel, 53, 69
reality
extra-temporal, as a Proustian concept, 6, 25, 32, 57, 64, 68, 111
as a theme, 12–16, 25, 29, 37, 46, 48–49, 65, 68, 81, 98
red shoes, incident of the, 21
religion, 6, 82–83

*Remembrance of Things
     Past*
  as autobiography, 4, 66,
     92, 94, 105–106
  chronology in, 4, 6, 12,
     56–57
  first-person narration in,
     3–4, 33, 45, 97–98
  literature in, 59; "life is
     literature," 80–81;
     See also: Balzac;
     Bergotte; St. Simon;
     Arabian Nights
  music in. *See:* Vinteuil
  narrative technique in,
     12–13, 20, 22, 56
  optical instruments in, 2,
     28, 85–86
  painting in, 11, 37, 38, 80.
     See also: Elstir
  parallel structure in, 16,
     50, 62
  Proust begins to write, 99
  publication of, 6, 28, 101–
     102
  structure of, 3–8, 19, 22,
     24–25, 56, 74–75, 79,
     102–103, 108
  themes of. *See:* art; death;
     habit; homosexuality;
     illusion; "intermit-
     tences of the heart";
     jealousy; love; mem-
     ory; mother's good-
     night kiss; prisoner;

     reality; snobbism;
     "successive selves";
     time; time lost;
     windows
Richard, Jean-Pierre, 109
Romains, Jules, 4
roman à clef, 4
roman fleuve, 4
rouge et le noir, Le
     (Stendhal), 110
Ruskin, John, 96–97

Sainte-Beuve, Charles Au-
     gustin, 98
Saint-Euverte, Mme. de, 21,
     61–62, 83
St. Loup, Mlle. de, 70–72,
     85
St. Loup, Marquise de
     (Gilberte), 57
St. Loup, Robert de, 17–18,
     47–48, 53, 68–71, 93
Saint-Saëns, Camille, 78
Saint-Simon, Duc de, 7, 109
Sand, George, 65
Scott Moncrief, C.-K., 5, 15
Sesame and Lilies (Ruskin),
     96
Shakespeare, William, 5
Shattuck, Roger, 85–86
snobbism, as a theme, 3, 19–
     21, 50, 107
society
  aristocratic, 19–21. *See
     also:* Guermantes

at Balbec, 14
the Baron and, 48–49, 94
Bergotte and, 76, 78
bourgeois, 19, 34–35. *See
    also:* Verdurin
changes in, 20, 69–70
Elstir and, 76, 78–79
the Marquise and, 19
the Narrator in, 19–20,
    66–72
Odette in, 76
Proust in, 94–95, 99–100
Proust's view of, 22,
    107–108
Mme. de Saint-Euverte
    and, 21
Swann in, 11, 29
Mme. Verdurin and, 21,
    34–35, 69, 76
See also: Faubourg St.
    Germain; snobbism
Sodom, 22–23, 25, 50, 75,
    107
*Sodome et Gomorrhe. See:
    Cities of the Plain*
Stein, Gertrude, 6, 111
Stendhal, 110
"successive selves"
Proust's theory of, 29–31,
    33, 38, 46, 48, 58,
    69, 76, 104
surrealism, 66
Swann, 9–13, 15, 17, 21, 24,

29–30, 32–39, 41–44,
    47–48, 50, 51, 53, 63,
    68, 70–72, 76, 85, 87,
    105–106
Swann in Love, 33, 38, 107
episodes of, 33–39
Swann's Way, 52, 74, 86, 99
episodes of, 8–13, 29–30,
    32–41, 72
publication of, 6, 28, 101–
    103
"Swann's Way" (as path
    and metaphor), 10,
    50, 57, 71
Sweet Cheat Gone, The, 41,
    56
episodes of, 46–48
symbolist movement, 7

Tansonville, 57, 103
*temps retrouvé, Le. See:
    Past Recaptured, The*
Théodore, 58
Third Republic, 3
*Thousand and One Nights,
    A*, 8, 109
time, as a theme, 4–6, 28, 30,
    40, 47, 56–58, 64–65,
    68, 72, 86, 111
See also: reality, extra-
    temporal
time lost, as a theme, 24,
    53–54, 59

Ulysses (Joyce), 111
uncle, the Narrator's, 30, 58,
    71

Vautrin, 49
Venice, 11, 29, 45, 48, 53, 63
Verdurin, Mme., 21, 34–35,
    37, 43, 50–52, 59–60,
    62, 70, 74, 76, 83
    and her "clan," 34–35
Verdurin, Mme. (*cont'd*)
  as Princesse de Guer-
    mantes, 69
Vermeer, Jan (of Delft), 76
Villeparisis, Marquise de,
    16–19, 29
Vinteuil, 22, 74, 76–78, 84,
    87
  septet by, 24, 74–75
  sonata by, 38, 74–75

Vinteuil, Mlle., 22, 43, 50,
    74–75
Vivonne river, 9, 57

Wagner, Richard, 35, 78
Wilde, Oscar, 94
windows, as a theme, 50,
    86–87
Within a Budding Grove,
    13, 15, 41
  episodes of, 12–17
  Goncourt Prize for, 102
  publication of, 102
Wolfe, Thomas, 112
Woolf, Virginia, 111
Wordsworth, William, 81
World War I, 52, 56, 60

Zola, Emile, 7